LOOK WITHIN

Change Your Thinking, Change Your Life

Gerry (Ged) Gleeson

LOOK WITHIN: Change Your Thinking, Change Your Life
© **Gerry** (Ged) **Gleeson 2019**

The moral rights of **Gerry Gleeson** to be identified as the author of this work have been asserted in accordance with the Copyright Act 1968

First published in **Australia 2019** by Gowor International Publishing

ISBN 978-0-6485885-0-4

Any opinions expressed in this work are exclusively those of the author and are not necessarily the views held or endorsed by Gowor International Publishing.

All rights reserved. No part of this publication may be reproduced or transmitted by any means, electronic, photocopying or otherwise, without prior written permission of the author.

Disclaimer
All the information, techniques, skills and concepts contained within this publication are of the nature of general comment only and are not in any way recommended as individual advice. The intent is to offer a variety of information to provide a wider range of choices now and in the future, recognising that we all have widely diverse circumstances and viewpoints. Should any reader choose to make use of the information herein, this is their decision, and the author and publisher/s do not assume any responsibilities whatsoever under any conditions or circumstances. The author does not take responsibility for the business, financial, p ersonal or other success, results or fulfilment upon the readers' decision to use this information. It is recommended that the reader obtain their own independent advice.

Dedicated to... the World.

Advance Praise For

LOOK WITHIN – Change Your Thinking, Change Your Life

Gerry's book provides an accessible path to living a happier and more meaningful life through practical daily recommendations (habits) that seek to elevate our mindfulness and de-mystify spirituality. Highly Recommend.

Jacqui Gabor
Health and Wellness Practitioner
Brisbane, Australia

Gerry is passionate about his message for us to harness the determination and courage required to understand the ways in which limiting self-belief and conditioning hinders our experience of happiness and contentment. In generously sharing his own practices and daily habits, Gerry encourages readers to embrace and to develop their own practice, and to move toward living a more authentic and contented life that is guided by the unique whispers of their own heart.

Ms Moira Leonard
Adelaide, South Australia.

Gerry your book is different from many of the books I have read on the subject of how to live a good life. Yours is an amazing book full of simple easy-to-follow advice for anyone who reads it and who then follows that advice to have a more peaceful, happy and contented life. You have made me aware Gerry, and I thank you for that. Good luck with your book.

Mr Bernie Lowe
Director, Lowe Enterprise, Sunshine Coast, Queensland. Australia.

Table Of Contents

Preface xi
Introduction 1
Chapter 1: What You're Looking For is Within You 14
Chapter 2 Belief Systems and Your Personal Environment ... 31
Chapter 3: Be Grateful and Accept That God Has
    Your Master Plan 44
Chapter 4: Lack of Awareness 56
Chapter 5: The Past is OUR Greatest Life Lesson 70
Chapter 6: The Ego and its Problems – Learn to Let Go 90
Chapter 7: My Daily Practice 111
Chapter 8: Affirmations and Teachings of Buddha 157
Chapter 9: Master Achievers 171
Chapter 10: Inviting Abundance into Your Life and
    Avoiding Health Imbalances 184
Conclusion 199
Resources 210
Acknowledgements 211
About the Author 213

Preface

Over my years of life on this magnificent planet, I have concluded that most of the books that I studied at secondary school and at university, were books designed to educate me on how to get a job, earn an income, pay bills, purchase material assets, etc. They were basically books written to demonstrate to me 'how to survive in the physical world' and of course, all were very important. However, the books from which I learnt about life, about what it is that is required for leading a joyful, healthy, fulfilling, contented and peaceful life, I only discovered through my own reading choices while on a personal journey of self-discovery. And as a result, I very much agree with Sarah ban Breathnach's quote in her wonderful book *Simple Abundance – A Day Book of Comfort & Joy*, first published in 1995, and that quote was:

'Reading good books is as essential to life as breathing.'

Let me briefly explain why I wrote this book. During the first week of January 2018 as I was reading from Sarah's above-titled book which I had been reading from for some five years, the following small piece of commentary for January 5th was like a 'lightbulb' going off in my brain, an explosion of white light/**awareness**! It incorporated Sarah's New Year resolution, being only the fifth day of a new year, and the amazing piece was this: *'Turn away from the world this year and begin to listen. Listen to the whispers of your heart. Look Within.'* Reading this short portion at that exact moment in time, was an extraordinary moment in my life!

I will never forget that moment in time as it has changed my life forever. I will be eternally grateful to Sarah ban Breathnach for those few life-changing words, and it confirmed to me why I agree with her that books are as essential as breathing. It was at that very moment that I knew, absolutely knew in my heart, that I had to write this book. What I had not realised at that time was that the ultimate title of my book was hidden within that same small piece! Subsequently, I have written this book to encourage and to demonstrate to you, the reader, the importance of learning to listen to your 'Inner Self', which is those whispers of your heart.

Preface

Happiness is an 'inside' job! What is your heart telling you? What is it that you want your life to be? The purpose of this book is to explain the need for each of us to learn this vital life skill of **Looking Within** in order to manifest into our lives that **lasting happiness, inner peace and contentment** that lies deep within each of us.

"The heart is your authentic compass". (Sarah ban Breathnach)

If you live and work from the heart then you are heading in the right direction. The heart is the true you, the authentic you, and one must learn the importance of following it to manifest **lasting happiness, inner peace and contentment** into one's life.

My mission then was to write a book that if only one person was to read it and adopt into their **daily** life the same ten simple habits which I have been practising for some fifteen years plus, then I will have assisted that one person, wherever they may be in the World, to positively change their thinking. Meaning that it would ultimately have changed their life and they would have manifested **lasting happiness, inner peace and contentment** into their **daily** living. That would then mean for me: mission accomplished!

I once read the following quote:

Look Within

"If you don't see the book on the shelf that you want, write it". – Beverly Cleary (Author)

That is what I did!

ENJOY the read.

Introduction

'The greatest discovery of any generation is that any human being can alter their life by altering their attitude.'
– (William James 1842-1910 - Philosopher)

'We must be willing to let go of the life that we've planned, so as to have the life that is waiting for us.'
– (Joseph Campbell)

As you read this book it is important that you keep an open mind and heart. The book is essentially a 'guide book' containing proven **daily habits** that will assist you, the reader, to become a superior person, firstly in your own life but also so that you can contribute to a better world for all. It is about the importance of learning to reflect on how you think, speak and act moment by moment, and to explore how you relate to others. It is about why each of us MUST learn to do the 'inner work' on our individual Self before we can achieve happiness and contentment in our life. As faith in our leaders continues to erode in many Western countries, millions of us are feeling increasingly isolated and cynical.

This book will introduce you to 10 simple **daily habits** that I have adopted into my **daily** living for some fifteen plus years now. Habits that when followed daily, regardless of who you are or where you are in your life journey, will develop into core beliefs, and ultimately lead to changed positive behaviour in your life too. Make no mistake, regardless of where we were born, each of us was bought into this world first to be **aware**, and second to be happy! The advertising media, together with business and governments of all persuasions, pressure us to stay self-focused, to worry about how we look, to be concerned with how others think of us, etc. They have subsequently 'conditioned' us to believe that to be successful in life you must accumulate as much material wealth as you can as some sense of security (a false sense!).

Being successful and having a sense of security and contentment is not simply just about having material wealth, but rather, it is also about having peace of mind and a contented heart. You will only achieve that if, in conjunction with accumulating your

Introduction

material wealth, you understand why it is crucial that one learn and practise **daily** the art of **Looking Within** and listening to those important *whispers of your heart*.

In Western society, the pursuit of material success could be referred to as 'the Westerner's disease', which is the society in which we currently live. We live in a society obsessed with materialism, basically 'materialism on steroids'. In the West at least, we seem to be fixated with hurtling through life pursuing what others, particularly the media, have conditioned us to believe will automatically manifest **lasting happiness, inner peace and contentment** into our lives simply by us having more and more material possessions and focusing on our external world.

However, this constant pursuit of acquiring more and more material wealth, in many instances, is proving to result in somewhat the opposite outcome. For example, we are currently living in a society where many of those who have accumulated much material wealth, stardom, social status, business success, etc. are experiencing a dramatic increase in cases of depression, stress-related diseases, premature deaths, drug and/or alcohol addiction, domestic violence, suicide and much, much more. I recently read the following quote from the Dalai Lama which puts this situation into some perspective: **'People were made to be loved. Things were made to be used. The chaos in the world today is because we love things and we use people.'** Brilliant characterisation would you agree?

For many years now I have keenly observed that most Western societies appear to have increasingly lost their way in relation to the fundamental values that their citizens require to live happy, healthy and fulfilling lives. I have observed through interacting with good people every day over a long period of time, together with studying and living the philosophies of numerous accomplished authors/mentors, that we have now developed a Western society where many materially successful individuals appear to still experience deep struggles in their lives, even after attaining social status, extensive material wealth, etc.

Ultimately, this constant grappling with life, I believe, can be diagnosed as being a result of what is going on inside the individual's head, how and what they are thinking, their attitude to the world around them, etc. Hence, this book: **Look Within – *Change Your Thinking, Change Your Life.***

Many of us have failed to do the 'inner work' required to understand and appreciate much of what is discussed in this book. Why is it that many who appear materially to have everything (e.g. multiple homes & motor vehicles, happy family

Introduction

life, good health, extensive stock portfolio's, large bank accounts, successful businesses, social status,) are the very same people who often are still discontent with life in general? The question then really becomes: Do they have what they need, or possibly crave, without being mentally **aware** of it which ultimately is <u>**lasting**</u> **happiness, inner peace and contentment?**

Most of what makes a good book is that we read it at a time that is the perfect moment in our life for us to read it. I have had that experience numerous times throughout my life. This book has been written to demonstrate why many who constantly strive to accumulate more and more 'material wealth' struggle to understand what living a meaningful, joyful, fulfilled, peaceful and contented life is all about.

Many are essentially not **aware** of what is required to manifest the <u>**lasting**</u> **happiness, inner peace and contentment** that all human beings desire. Instead of allowing the outside world to tell you how to live, what your values and beliefs should be, what to fear, etc. You must learn to listen to and be guided by what your heart is telling you. You must listen to *the whispers of your heart*. And to do that, you must learn to constantly, **Look Within**. People have worked hard and/or built businesses, saved hard, invested well, etc. all to get to a point in life where they should be content and relaxed about their life, only to discover that they still have this yearning, this longing if you like, that something is missing.

This book is a blueprint to show how one can overcome, or better still avoid, this world-wide problem from developing in their life. If you resolve to work each day to transform **'how you think'**, you are totally honest with yourself and your heart is open to change, then the mind will follow and positive, personal transformation will be the ultimate outcome.

Many of the things that we have chosen to believe about ourselves have absolutely no basis in truth. They have been based on what others say or think of us, not necessarily on what we say or think of our Self. If you don't currently like your life as it is right now, then just start making better choices. One such choice may be to adopt into your life the simple **DAILY HABITS** as set-out in this book You choose the life you live, so if you don't like it, then it's up to YOU to change it. No one else can do that for you. This is your journey. And always remember that famous quote, regardless of your age: **If it is to be, then it's up to me.**

Unless you change how you think and act, then you are bound to keep manifesting the same outcomes. Zig Ziglar once famously said: **'If you always do as you have always done, then you will always get what you have always got.'** In other words,

Introduction

if you do not change your thinking and/or your behaviour, then you are always going to achieve the same or similar outcomes to those that you have been currently manifesting in your life. Hence the subtitle of this book: *Change Your Thinking, Change Your Life.* This is just basic common sense when you take the time to stop and think deeply on this proposition! And that is what this book is about: the importance of **Looking Within**, doing the 'inner work', changing how you think about life and then, as a result of all this activity, experience your life, changing!

The next time that you think that you are having a bad day, a bad week, month or year, or something has not worked out the way that you had planned for it to go, just open this book at the picture shown in the first pages of the book. A picture of hundreds and hundreds of human beings just like you and me, fleeing their war-torn, destroyed homes and businesses in Syria! So **STOP, PAUSE, and REFLECT** here for a few minutes and think about that!

How bad are your present-day circumstance really, whatever they may be, when compared to these people who have lost everything, including for many their own life or that of a loved one, sometime shortly after this picture was taken? **PLEASE,** think deeply about this reality for a few minutes! That picture is a snapshot of the real everyday world that we currently live in. When I first saw this picture in a newspaper some years ago, it had such a powerful impact on me to the point that I immediately photo-copied the picture, took it to a photo-print shop and had several copies of it laminated and printed off in A4 size. My motivation for doing this was so that I could refer to this graphic picture every morning in my 15-20 minutes of quiet reflection time. I subsequently quickly realised that this **daily habit**/practise *Changed My Thinking,* which subsequently *Changed My Life.*

From time to time we all have challenges and that will continue. We must all accept that challenges are an important part of living our lives. What can change though is our perception of what those challenges mean. Challenges are no more than life lessons. Our attitude and how we deal with the challenges we face is just a way of God/Spirit/Source/? messaging us. Our greatest battles in life will always be internal. Any demons that we may have are demons that reside in our minds, in how and what we think. This is our whole of life challenge, to continually learn, to change, and to grow internally from our difficulties. **Personal transformation begins with us developing a strong 'inner life'.** Happiness, peace and contentment, as well as our despair, arises from the Mind. From **Within!** When we are seeking lasting happiness and an end to our suffering or struggles, the initial place to look for solutions must be from **Within**.

And that, my friend, is what this book is about. Learning the importance of constantly **Looking Within**. God/Spirit/Source/? will find it quite difficult to pass information and guidance to you if you are constantly moving, thinking, talking or working at something. That is why you will see the following words **STOP, PAUSE, REFLECT** appear many times throughout the book because it is vital, that the reader does exactly that to allow the messages that they have just received/read to resonate with them on a deep level. On a Soul level.

Affirm:

I am open to receiving all the abundance and blessings I deserve.

You can attract more of what you want in life by first and foremost choosing to learn more about yourself. To do that you must learn the skill of **Looking Within** and then practise this <u>**daily!**</u> This book will provide you with simple <u>daily habits</u> that you can adopt into YOUR life and thereby, you can discover your very own pathway to <u>**lasting happiness, inner peace and contentment**</u>. Many spend a lifetime searching for this, but sadly, they never discover that the whole time it was **Within** them!

They never learnt to **LOOK WITHIN**.

'After all, it is those who have a deep and real inner life who are best able to deal with the irritating details of the outer life.'
– (Evelyn Underhill)

There is nothing wrong with pursuing material success and financial independence. That can be, and is, a good thing. But do not allow this striving for material success to shift from your passion to become an obsession. Remember always that ultimate success in YOUR life comes from following those **whispers of your heart,** whatever they may be, and they are different for each of us. One just needs to honestly look into their heart and ask themselves what it is that is truly important to them as an individual and then view the world with new eyes. One way to attract more of what you need in your life is by choosing to educate yourself more about exactly what it is that YOU want.

Studying/learning from books like this one can be a good starting point. Life rewards those who have courage, take risks, break out from their fears and act. If you have fears about what lies ahead, just feel those fears and do it anyway. Fear is often nothing more than **f**alse **e**vidence **a**ppearing **r**eal! Remember, as I expressed earlier, to move ahead in your life: **reading good books is as essential as breathing is to life!**

Introduction

'A home with a large Library is a wonderful home to be in.'
– (Robin Sharma)

Many invest much time and make financial commitments for life-changing training programs, seminars, webinars, etc. to educate themselves on how to achieve financial success and independence. This is highly commendable, but people tend to invest little if any time, energy or money on educating themselves on developing their 'spiritual **awareness**'. We are all made up of three elements: **body, mind and spirit**. We need to understand and accept why it is critical that we invest time, energy and money on learning the importance of having all three elements developing in balance if we desire **lasting happiness, inner peace and contentment** in our life.

It can help to think of it along the following lines. Think of a three-room home where Room 1 is the Body, Room 2 is the Mind, and Room 3 is the Spirit. We need to work on (spend time in) each room (part of our makeup) daily. Over time, if we neglect having worked on the body, mind and spirit then just like a physical room that we do not spend time in, dust, cobwebs, darkness, etc. take-over. And to maintain optimum physical, mental and spiritual health, we need to devote time **daily** to the Body, the Mind and to our Spirit.

<u>Buddha:</u>

'The Greatest Weakness in Life is Lack of Awareness.'

'The Greatest Enemy in Life is the SELF.'

Chapter 1:
What You're Looking for is 'Within You'

'All that you need is deep within you waiting to unfold and reveal itself. All that you have to do is to be still and take time to seek for what is within, and you will surely find it.'
– (Eileen Caddy)

Buddha believed that the greatest enemy that we face in our life is our very own self. We can be, and often are, our own worst enemy. To accept this universal fact requires both intense courage and honesty. This is a statement of truth that can be confronting and may well challenge you. It requires real courage to be open and honest with one's Self, and to not deceive or deny one's emotions when participating in such soul-searching. One must not allow pride, guilt or self-pity to obscure the good qualities that each of us has deep within our 'Inner-self'. Many are unable to accept that how we think, speak and act can and often is our worst enemy in life.

STOP, PAUSE, REFLECT now for a few minutes on this very important point, because it is a universal truth. Without realising it, we can be our own worst enemy. This book is about providing a platform for you to accept and deal with this universal truth and to provide a pathway to introduce into your **daily** life a practice to help change how and what you think, resulting in you manifesting that **lasting happiness, inner peace and contentment** that we all so desire.

Over many years now, I have concluded, along with other inspired people, that most of us generally live in this world doing everything back the front. We have been 'conditioned' from a very young age that it is very important to work hard, to be materially successful and to strive to acquire many of those symbols of success according to our so-called modern world (e.g. more money, better social status, more cars, more houses, more clothes, more, more, more) and then we will be happy.

Author and spiritual mentor Dr Wayne Dyer once wrote: 'The purpose of life was just to be happy. To enjoy life. To let God, and just allow.' Unfortunately, we have been 'conditioned' from this very young age to believe that if you continually strive to have more material wealth then ultimately you will be successful, happy and content. However, it is somewhat the reverse that leads to **lasting happiness, inner peace and contentment**. It is not that having material wealth is of itself a bad thing, it is not. We should all strive to acquire and enjoy many of the magnificent material gifts that the universe has to offer to us. That is not the problem. What many of us fail to realise and accept though on a deep level, on a Soul level, is that enduring happiness, inner peace and contentment can only come from '**within**' one's Self.

We must understand and accept that we individually need to foster a 'balance' between our material goals or pre-occupation and our spiritual growth and development, which need not necessarily be based on any traditional religious faith. You do however need to make a commitment to enhance your 'spiritual values' and to be a kind, warm-hearted, compassionate person. Lasting happiness must be pursued on a mental level and not just from the outside material world. From the contents of this book, you will come to understand and accept the importance of this concept on your very own pathway to **lasting happiness, inner peace and contentment**. One can never just go out and purchase lasting happiness. For example, regardless of your material wealth, one cannot buy genuine, sincere love! Many have tried, but it is well documented that it does not last.

Initially, much of what you have read so far may be difficult to accept, given that lasting happiness, inner peace and contentment are what most of us are searching for, striving for, or worse still, craving. And craving anything is suffering. Therefore, we need to develop a mindset that craves or clings to nothing. It is this clinging (**attachment**) to a specific person, place, thing or feeling that Buddhist's believe is the cause of all suffering. This is another universal truth! We all so easily become connected to particular people, animals, objects and places. This of itself is not the problem, but rather, it is our attachment to them that causes the suffering!

More and more we are discovering that acquiring objects that we **desire** rather than **need**, is not necessarily leading to the lasting happiness and contentment that we had hoped for and have been conditioned to expect, particularly by the media (including all social media) and the advertising industry. Hence, we are constantly looking for our next purchase of some material object or our next 'fix' if you like, to make us happy. Many of us are hooked on this crazy treadmill of wanting, wanting, wanting! It is this obsession with seeking happiness, contentment and peace of mind from *outside* of our 'Inner Self' that causes so much of our mental anguish, stress and pain, even to the point where many of us can develop serious behavioural problems and illnesses as a result (e.g. depression, cancer, domestic and other forms of violence, etc.)

It is why so many in our society turn to spontaneous and excessive consumer spending, illegal drugs, risky alcohol consumption, prescription medications, violence and suicide. They are less and less able to cope with their perceived lack of hope of ever achieving that lasting happiness, inner peace and contentment that we all desire. We must learn and accept, that fulfilment in our life can only come from **'within'** and not from simply acquiring more and more of these external symbols of success. This book is a 'guide book' to help you to realise, to accept, and to live this universal truth <u>**daily**</u> that:

<u>Lasting</u> happiness, peace and contentment, can only come from Within!

Therefore, first and foremost we must learn, yes that's right regardless of our age, first and foremost we must **learn** to be who we really are as individuals. When we stop blaming others for where we are at in our life and for what is happening in our life here in the present, it is then and only then that we will regain our personal power. Why is it that most of us spend so much of our time focusing on what we do not have in our lives and so little time focusing on what we do have. Why is that?

What You're Looking for is 'Within You'

STOP, PAUSE, REFLECT on this very statement for a few minutes.

Worse, why is it that many often tend to focus on what others have rather than focusing their thoughts on what they have in their own life right now and for which they should be grateful every day? Why is it that so many of us choose to live that way? You will learn from reading this book that as you practise gratitude (the art of **daily** being grateful) then you will become more **aware**, more present. *You will wake up!*

I remember attending a multi-level marketing seminar many years ago with approximately 300 other individuals-and I listened to an extraordinary speaker who towards the end of his session almost pleaded with the audience to listen to his closing remarks. Imagine that you are there in that audience right now. There is deathly silence, and this speaker is virtually pleading to you the following advice.

"If you give up on your dreams if you quit! If you let the dreams you have for your life just fade away. If you just give up. Then you will become part of what I call the 'zombie generation'! You just become part of the masses who get up, go to work, come home, sleep. Get up, go to work, come home, sleep. Get up, go to work, come home, sleep. On and on it goes for years and years! You are just part of this zombie generation. Your life just passes you by. Please, please, NEVER give up on your dreams," he

pleaded to us all. You could have heard a pin drop in that room, as his pleading voice had captivated everyone with that message. I have never forgotten these comments and it is why as you look around today you can easily conclude that many of our fellow citizens are not really living at all. They are drifting through life like zombies. That is why we all continuously MUST accept the need to first **Look Within** when we feel a need to change how we are presently living.

Why is it that even if many achieve much material wealth, financial freedom, good health, social status, a life partner, children, etc. they still have this yearning deep within them that there is something missing in their life? And why, sadly, do we continue to search outside of ourselves for the answers when all along the answers reside **within**. Has anything from the world outside of your 'Inner Self' ever bought you lasting happiness, inner peace and contentment? The emphasis here is on **lasting!**

There is nothing wrong with having all or any of these symbols of material wealth and success: money, houses, stocks, cars, boats, social status, etc. However, it is our 'attachment' to them that creates anxiety and stress because they all tend to come and go. People come and go in our life, money comes and goes, nothing remains permanent. Hence, when

What You're Looking for is 'Within You'

we lose any or all of them, we can end up feeling empty and disillusioned inside. We need balance in our work/social life.

For an excellent example of balance, think gardeners. My darling wife Liz is a passionate gardener who constantly talks about how a garden must have balance in relation to its structural layout, how the plants are arranged, etc. Yet, at the same time, as we may strive to ensure balance in our gardens, we can easily neglect the need for balance in our personal life, career, marriage, other relationships, etc. And for all of us, just like gardens, if we do not have good foundations (**Beliefs, Values, Faith**) then our personal development and growth will suffer just like the plants in a garden.

Nature is a classic example of being in balance. Without humans on this planet, Mother Nature today would always be in perfect balance just as she was before humans inhabited the Earth. We feed our gardens nutrients, water, fertilisers, etc. for the plants to grow and so similarly, we need to feed our 'Inner Self'. We need to feed our Soul, with inner growth supplements like study, meditation, nourishing food, exercise, love, laughter, etc We also need to take time **daily** to reflect and to give Thanks. Time to be grateful! The human body needs to be nourished **daily,** physically, emotionally and spiritually. *Inner growth and development are as important to each of us as breathing is to life.*

Breathing air into our lungs is something that we do automatically, subconsciously whereas inner growth is something that you either freely choose to do or not to do. That is one of the many freedoms that each of us has, the freedom to choose. Currently, many humans are 'spiritually starved', not physically underfed, but rather spiritually undernourished! And that is due to the fact, I believe, that a large part of the problem for many who struggle with life is because they have chosen to not read and learn from good books once they have finished in the traditional school education systems and entered the workforce.

We need to wake up to the importance of continuing with our learning from good books and to understand and accept that this practice is vital for our ongoing physical and mental wellbeing. We must all, regularly: **Stop. Read. Listen. Learn and Grow.**

Remember: 'The greatest enemy in life is the self.' – (Buddha)

It is vital that one nourishes one's 'Inner Self' (the Soul) regularly, preferably **daily**, with spiritual and emotional food (good books, etc.) just as one needs to consume food daily to sustain a healthy body. To achieve **lasting happiness, inner peace and contentment** in our life we need to practise nurturing an *inner life* rather than just concentrating exclusively on the outer trappings. Enjoy and practise the processes that you will learn from this book and reap the benefits. When the balance in our **daily** lives is askew, then just like in our gardens, all areas of our life suffer. Often it can take an unscheduled event in our lives to awaken us to the need to maintain balance in our personal life e.g. a health scare, the death of a loved one, a child being bullied, losing a business or job, etc.

'Turn away from the world this year and begin to listen. Listen to the whispers of your heart. Look Within.'

STOP, PAUSE, REFLECT right now, and regardless of the time of the year, think deeply again on that statement. It is a very powerful statement indeed if you are a 'seeker' of a more profound meaning to life than just that which the material trappings of our world have to offer. You need to take the time to just tune out from the world, switch off the world of the 'thinking mind' and take time out to just *Be*. Think of your Mind being like a monkey, that as we know continually just jumps crazily from place to place!

Therefore, to discover who you really are, first, you must **PAUSE**. Yes, you need to just **PAUSE** from the madness of this rushing outer world and find inner stillness. What I mean by that is you MUST find 15-20 minutes at least, **daily**, to just **STOP** doing. Sit quietly alone somewhere without all the digital gadgets, television, Facebook, Instagram, Twitter, newspapers, work projects, etc. and take an open, honest look at YOU, internally.

This is not about giving up on your goals or dreams and joining the 'zombie generation', but rather it is learning the importance of becoming **aware** of what ultimately matters in your precious life, which is to live your life as you want your life to be. It means turning off all negativity. It's funny you know, but I have discovered that if you are always grateful for something, no matter how small (e.g. having a pulse!), then you cannot be negative! Let go of any toxic/negative people in your life. Let go of the past. Let go of regrets and the need to be right that we all experience at various stages in our lives. Let's not be pushed around by our fears or the fears of others. Be **aware** that fear is just False Evidence **A**ppearing **R**eal (F.E.A.R.). Be led in your life by your dreams, and the only place where your dreams become impossible to manifest is **within** your thinking.

Before we can expect anything in our lives to change, regardless of our present circumstances, we must **STOP** and do a detailed and critically honest assessment of our 'Inner Self'. This is not always easy and can be somewhat confronting and challenging. But it is imperative that we be very honest with this important first step. If we are not totally open and totally honest with this self-examination process, then the only person that we are ultimately cheating is our very own Self. Think about that! We must, I will repeat that, we must learn to *look inward* and ask the question:

'Am I living a life of abundance or a life limited by the conditions imposed by my mind and by the thoughts of others.'

STOP, PAUSE, REFLECT on that statement for a few moments before you continue reading

The human mind, and listening to the opinions of others, puts 'conditions' on how we live. Think of very young children. Often, even now, when I am having fun, friends will look at me with a strange expression on their face as if to silently signal to me 'don't you think you should grow up?' And my internal response to that look as I smile is, why should kids have all the fun! This is the attitude that I have had about life for as long as I can remember, and it is a classic example where one becomes **aware** of an important key on how to live life.

Many of us have forgotten how to have fun. Many have forgotten how to laugh and why it's important to laugh and to laugh often! Laughter is an excellent medicine for the Body, Mind and the Spirit. Sadly, too many of us spend too much time clinging onto past behaviours, or we tend to live our life based on what others may think of us if we act in a certain way. All one needs to do is regularly just sit and observe very young children. When they are playing and having fun, they do not care for an instant what others may say or think of them, they just do! They are fully engaged. They are in the zone! They are having fun. They do not think of or hang onto their past. They hold no grudges. They live in the present moment! They do not just exist, they are not zombies, they LIVE for today! Unfortunately, that is until the adult 'conditioning' kicks in!

I remember watching an excellent Dr Wayne Dyer YouTube video some years ago during which he explains what he believes happens when we are first born. He put it like this: when we are in the mother's womb for that first nine months of our physical development and the creation of all our body parts, God is in complete control of that process. But the moment that this new human is born, the parents reach for the tiny baby and say something along these lines "Thank you God for creating and handing us this beautiful little human being, we will take over now!"

And that is exactly what happens! The well-meaning parents, and others, immediately take over caring for and raising this child, as it should be, but it is at this exact moment that the life-long 'conditioning' process also commences. The 'Egos' of the parents and others now come to the fore and as the 'Ego' stands for Edging **G**od **O**ut (**E.G.O.**), this is precisely what happens. The small child knows that we are here to enjoy all the gifts that God/Spirit/Source/? has made available to us, to have fun, to enjoy whatever we desire, etc. but our well-meaning parents and others start to control how and what we think! They put limitations on what we can strive for by saying things like "Gee, we think that would be too hard for you…" or "We don't think that would look right for you…" or "Mum and Dad think you should be an accountant, or a lawyer, we know what's best for you son/daughter" etc.

You regularly comply and do this or that according to their wants instead of your own, and often you comply just to keep the peace and/or to stay out of trouble. **The conditioning has commenced!** Parents and others, unwittingly I must stress, did the best that they could, acting on what they knew at the time from their own life experiences, but it can and often does stunt or stem our personal development right from day one. They no doubt meant well and acted from a place of love, but unfortunately, they have instigated that life long process for many of us individuals to believe (belief systems) that we are not capable or not good enough, to live the life that we aspire to live.

And so, we tend to live a life that has been mapped out for us by our parents and others rather than living the life that we dreamed to live. However, now that you are **aware** of this, possibly for the very first time, you can do something about it. From this day forward, you can work at changing this situation and begin living that life that you aspire to. It is never too late. For example, the late Lois Hay changed her thoughts at around the age of 60, commenced writing books, and even launched what has gone on to become the incredibly successful publishing house, Hay House. One is never too old, or too young for that matter, to change how one thinks. One needs only to learn the importance of regularly practising that principle of **Looking Within.**

We need to understand how and what we currently think, change that thinking and then practise such transformed thinking, <u>**daily**</u>. This book has been written with that sole objective, to help you to adopt this life-changing process and to develop vital <u>**daily habits**</u>. If you choose to change how you think, speak and act, then your whole world changes. Your life changes! This can be a challenge that requires real courage, honesty and trust. A new you is born and the old you is 'let go'. But it does require you to firstly choose, and then to commit to and to do that 'inner' work, so that your new Self can emerge.

Many limit themselves by having and maintaining closed minds. Pride or fear of what others may think, can often make it difficult for them to accept a need for change in their daily living patterns of how they are choosing to live. Some are unaware of this need to change how they think and act until a crisis overtakes them. Positive change does not come quickly or overnight, and it demands ongoing effort and commitment. However, with a persistent and determined application for positive change, one can accomplish the most difficult of objectives.

I KNOW THAT IN EACH MOMENT I AM FREE TO DECIDE.

Chapter 2:
Belief Systems & Your Personal Environment

"I know that I am already whole and that I need not chase after anything in order to be complete."
– (Author Unknown)

This quote mandates that you MUST take at least 15-20 minutes **daily**, preferably first thing in the morning, to just sit quietly anywhere that you like and to think deeply on what it is that YOU believe in (i.e. your Beliefs and Faith), what values you have, how and what you think, how you speak and the words that you use, what you eat, how you exercise and look after your health, whether you take full responsibility for what you say and for your actions, whether you judge others, whether you have expectations, are you compassionate, who you associate with, are you **<u>daily</u>** grateful and thankful for all that you have, and much, much more.

It is only when in this space of inner stillness that messages will flow to you and you will become **aware**, possibly for the very first time, that each of us has the power to discover our purpose or passion. We must ask ourselves: What is it that we really want from our life? And it is vital in this process to always be completely open and honest with one's Self as honesty is an essential prerequisite for looking deeply **within**, and to becoming **aware** as to the truth of what is important for living a fulfilling life. You must recognise and accept on a deep inner level who you are right now in the present, before you can move forward with renewed confidence and self-esteem.

Do not worry about who you think others think you are, but who YOU think and know yourself to be to your core, and more importantly, who YOU want to be! To achieve the richest of benefits from your life, I suggest that this learning process will work best for those who approach it with an open heart and mind, willingness, commitment and humility. The process requires not only that you be critically open and honest with yourself, but it also requires great courage.

You *MUST* accept as fact that it is your current 'belief systems' that automatically cause you to act in a certain way. In other words, it is your **'belief systems'** that determine your actions in the relationships you attract, the health you experience, the industry that you work in and the happiness you exude. Your beliefs are who YOU are right now, here in the present moment! Unfortunately, as stated in the previous chapter, we have been conditioned, 'socially conditioned', from birth by others to believe that we have limitations on what we can and cannot achieve in life. We must find the courage to 'let go' of such beliefs and re-write our own agreement with reality i.e. what we perceive to be possible for our Self.

To achieve such an outcome, we must shift out of our old beliefs that have been handed to us from someone outside of our Self e.g. a parent, a teacher, work colleagues, friends, etc. and develop our very own beliefs. We must simply 'let go' of what others think and believe and turn our attention **inward** to what our Self thinks, believes, needs or wants. This process begins with a thought, which is a simple choice that we freely make at any time of the day.

You must learn to believe that on that deep **inner** level what you think about is what can and will manifest into your life. And one of the happiest moments in your life will be when you find the courage to 'let go' of what you cannot control or change.

'The key to happiness is being aware that you have in any moment, the power to choose what to accept and what to 'let go'.' – (Dodinsky)

Take a couple of 'Letting Go' breaths right now and contemplate this concept.

BREATH – RELAX – LET GO

A belief is just a thought that we think about repeatedly. It is simply a **habit** of having that same thought until we do not even think it anymore, it is just a part of who we have become in the present moment. Therefore, we need to practise and repeat to our Self the following as often as we can: *From this day forward, I am totally responsible for my own life, I no longer live my life based on what anyone else thinks or says about me.*

Now that is power. Personal power! You are then living at a higher level of consciousness than when you relied on the opinions, beliefs or the approval of others. You are now the master of your own destiny. When you are living **daily** at this higher level of **awareness**, you automatically choose to practise being kind, rather than being right, for that is when you are at peace.

'You are the average of the 5 people with whom You spend most of your time.'

Belief Systems & Your Personal Environment

It is our personal environment that creates our 'belief systems'. Hence, we need to choose our environment carefully. In this context, 'environment' means those with whom we associate for most of our time.

STOP, PAUSE, REFLECT and think about that for a few minutes. It is very important that we are **aware** that to be the person that we want to be, we must take care when choosing (and we always have the freedom to choose) with whom we spend the vast bulk of our time. Remember those early years of your life. Maybe the five people with whom you spent most of your time back then, as it was for me, would be close family, particularly your parents.

As children, your parents had enormous influence in your life and in you developing your beliefs. It is in those early years when our 'belief systems' are initially developing that family are normally the most significant influencers. Then as we move forward in time, it would be our teachers, other students, employers, work colleagues, new friends, relationships, the media, etc. Also, in those early years when we never had the opportunity to freely choose our beliefs, our **'belief systems'** developed based on what our parents, uncles and aunties, and those mentioned above believed. And their 'belief systems' were passed down from a generation before them, whose belief systems were developed from a generation before them, and on and on it goes.

We didn't even get to choose our own name! We are often not who we believe we are because we never chose our own core beliefs. However, having said that, there are many valuable beliefs and values that have been passed onto us by our peers, including having respect first and foremost for our Self, and then respect for all others. We were taught to be personally responsible for all that we say and for how we act and to be respectful of others. We learned the importance of being kind, considerate and to show compassion for all, particularly for the less fortunate, etc.

So, until now we have lived our lives based on what others believed in for too long, like striving for material wealth at the expense of others, striving for power, developing self-image and social status, being separate and selfish rather than being inclusive and community-minded, etc. We have lost touch with our very own inner wisdom. We have unwittingly given various people in our lives power over us. We may not have been **aware** until now that it is these 'belief systems' that were created for us by others and that we have just blindly followed, which may be still controlling or influencing our lives today. And they are beliefs that are generally based on fear, which is really nothing more than **False Evidence Appearing Real (F.E.A.R)**.

Fear is a paralyser. Do not fear change. To 'let go' and move forward in your life sometimes requires that you may well have to 'let go' of some of your present company and allow new people to enter your life. You must learn the importance of being able to 'let go' of the toxic or negative people that you may presently have in your life. Letting go is not always easy, but it will be rewarding in the long term.

Learn to trust the true 'whisperings' of your **inner being**, those whispers of your heart! Sit quietly, alone, and explore those unknown parts of your inner being, as there is personal power in the process of participation. In fact, participation is the most powerful tool that we have for change. In this process of participating, we can change situations in ways that we could never have previously imagined and thereby create powerful change **within** ourselves. Participation, full participation, is not about control. You are what YOU think/believe you are, not what someone else thinks/believes you are.

Change your beliefs and attitude and you change your life. Hence the subtitle of this book: ***Change Your Thinking, Change Your Life***. Open your arms and heart to change, but do not let go of your values. And always remember: Reward follows effort!

'It matters little what others say or think of me, it matters much what I say and think of myself.'
– (Oscar Wilde)

My philosophy on life is just that! I am what I am. I try to always have no expectations and I accept everything that comes my way, because I believe and accept that a Higher Power is ultimately in control! And that is exactly what makes life so much easier and helps to manifest <u>lasting</u> happiness, inner peace and contentment in my life.

Much personal suffering often comes from believing that you are responsible for what other people say or think of you. But it is the opposite that is true! The only thing that matters in YOUR life, always, is what you say and think of yourself! **It is vital that you understand and accept this universal truth!** However, it naturally follows that if we want to be accepted as we are then we must also be willing to accept others as they are. Acceptance is just giving our Self and others the ability to just Be. To just be who they are, no judgement! Make it a Rule in your life: *to make no judgements.*

It is imperative that you learn this truth and that it becomes a permanent part of who you are: **'It matters little what others say or think of me. It matters much what I say and think of myself.'** I express this quote numerous times throughout the book for this very reason. Learn to repeat it to yourself as often as you can until it becomes a part of your normal thought processes. Part of your **'Inner Self'**!

STOP, PAUSE, REFLECT on this very important fact for a few minutes before you continue reading.

If you accept what you have just read, and I sincerely hope that you do, then now that you are **aware** of this imposed situation, you can take control, change, and develop your very own *'belief system'*. A belief system that will define who you are right now in the present moment! When we are **aware** and accept unconditionally that we are a product of our 'environment' (i.e. who we hang out with), it requires real courage and commitment to then change those old *'belief systems'* and to lead our lives based on our newly acquired beliefs. We must accept that we are always responsible for the consequences of whatever we think, say, do and feel. It is our choice!

Remember this quote that I wrote in large print a few pages earlier: **'I know that in each moment I am free to decide.'** We are free to choose who we are and what we believe! In most Western societies, each of us has this wonderful gift, the gift that is the freedom to choose. And it is our beliefs, freely chosen, that determine our existence. We are no longer going to be a victim of past 'belief systems' that were forced on to us by others because we are now aware that we oversee our own destiny.

The more we practise self-acceptance and this freedom to choose, the easier it becomes to shift away from **habits**/practises/choices that no longer serve us. However, it is very important to remember that we can only change how we think, say, do and feel. We cannot change others. Your happiness does not depend on your parents, your partner, your friends, your job or your past. It depends entirely on YOU!! Your life will be bigger when you stop worrying about what other people think or say about you in all situations. Just be who YOU choose to be!

Stay focused on what really matters — being your authentic Self! The real you. Be who you want to be, not who others want you to be. It is important, however, at this early stage of your new beginnings, that you be careful and don't attempt imposing these new thought processes that you are learning about here onto others. During the early weeks and months of adopting the practices outlined in this book, gently and quietly do this *'inner work'* on yourself before you share with others who may not necessarily want you to change and grow.

You may well experience difficult, confronting and challenging periods ahead as you adopt into your days the practices and **daily habits** as outlined in this book. In time, however, you will come to understand why this caution is important at this time. Trust me!

Acclaimed Australian author Bronnie Ware, who for a number of years worked privately with dying people as a palliative care nurse, wrote in her first book, *The Top Five Regrets of the Dying*, that the number one regret of dying people was this: **'I wish I'd had the courage to live a life true to myself and not the life others expected of me.'** So, let's not wait until you are dying to learn that lesson. Let's learn that lesson now and start living a life of being true to yourself in the present. Starting right now, today! Your 'life-clock' is ticking. *Tick tock, tick tock, tick tock… Time is ticking away!*

BEGIN TODAY OBSERVING YOUR BEHAVIOUR PATTERNS

I CHOOSE TO LIVE MY LIFE IN THE PRESENT MOMENT AND APPRECIATE IT FOR WHAT IT IS – *'A PRECIOUS GIFT'*

Chapter 3:
Be Grateful and Know that God has Your Master Plan

'I know that my Higher Self (Spiritual Self) is always ready to lift me up beyond the world that I experience with my senses.'
– (Author Unknown)

We need to learn and accept that no matter what plans and goals we may have for our life that ultimately, God/Spirit/Source/? has our 'Master Plan'!

Question: Do you want to know how to make God laugh? Answer: tell him about *YOUR* plans!

STOP, PAUSE, REFLECT on that for a few moments before you read on.

It is important for us to have dreams, goals, plans, etc. so long as we accept that ultimately God/Spirit/Source/? has the **'Master Plan'** for each of us! Often when people are faced with a tough situation in their life, you will notice that they pray, some for the very first time, and they tend to pray along the following lines, for example, "Please God, help me to get this job that I applied for" or "Please God, help this medical procedure to go well for me" or "Please God, help this business that I am starting-up to be successful" or whatever it may be that they want. Almost pleading with God for His help!

When one should really take a slightly more realistic approach with a slight change and ASK for help along these lines for these same examples above: "Dear God, I pray that it is part of **Your plan** for me that I will get this job that I have applied for" or "Dear God, I pray that it is part of **Your plan** for me that this medical procedure will go well" or "Dear God, I pray that it is part of **Your plan** for me that this business that I am starting-up is successful" etc.

Notice that when praying in this manner, we are ASKING for whatever it is that we want to be a part of God's Plan for us. We ask in this way and hand the outcome over to God. Do we always get what we ask for? Probably not, that is unless it is within **God's Master Plan** for us. We must learn to accept the outcome, whatever it may be, and then move on. Everything has a reason or purpose. So, the procedure is: we Ask, we Act, we Detach from the outcome. We Let Go and Let God. We must trust that whatever the outcome, even though we may not understand or appreciate it, it is ultimately always in our long-term best interest.

Let me give you a couple of personal examples of God having the **Master Plan**. When I was 12 years old, I suffered from a health problem known as rheumatic fever, which in this instance also included me grappling with a serious heart murmur. I was at that time in my life a very sick young boy. Part of my treatment, apart from the medications during a month in hospital, was that I was confined to bed 24/7, not allowed to have a pillow, not allowed to sit up, I could not feed myself or get out of bed to go to the toilet and I had to lay completely flat and as still as possible at all times. No easy task for someone so young.

However, I must have been at an age where I knew enough and was **aware** (or was God in control here?) to realise that if I wanted to get better then I must do exactly as my doctor instructed. Fortunately, I somehow managed to successfully comply with all that I was instructed to do. Whilst confined to that hospital bed, there was another young boy approximately six or seven years of age in that very same room who had identical health issues. Unfortunately, this young boy did not follow his doctor's instructions for he would jump out of bed and run around the ward as often as he could. My doctor (God's messenger?) pointed out to me at an early stage that this little boy would be a very sick individual later in life because he was not resting his heart as instructed and as he needed to do. Eventually, I was discharged from hospital and was confined to bed at home for a further period before making a full recovery after approximately six months in all.

Some years later, I came across this same young boy described above at my secondary school and I vividly remember how shocked I was at how sickly he looked in our school uniform, out playing in the schoolyard. This young boy passed away at around the age of fourteen years. However, I have gone on to lead a full and healthy life. Why did God choose to take that boy and not me? We never get to know the answer to the why because we do not get to see **God's Master Plan**, we just get to live it!

The second personal example of God having the Master Plan was when I was in my early thirties and I had been struggling for some years with terrible pain in both feet. I had tried various prescription drugs and monthly penicillin injections (bad idea!) over some years and arrived at a point that my doctor at the time (not any longer!) referred me to a Rheumatologist for further treatment. What was involved here was that I visited this specialist doctor who after a 10-minute consultation advised me that "You have arthritis and you will have to learn to live with it!" Can you believe that? A doctor just telling an otherwise fit and healthy early thirty-year-old person that 'they just have to learn to live with it'. He writes out a prescription for medication, hands it to me and then dismisses me and calls for his next patient.

As I am walking out of his room, his next patient, a young girl around 12-15 years old and her mother, move forward and enter his room. I vacate this medical centre and drop the prescription into the chemist shop downstairs and go for a coffee whilst the prescription is being made-up. I can clearly still remember much of what happened that day many years ago. When I finished that coffee and collected the medication, I stood frozen in a state of shock outside the chemist shop as the bottle full of the prescribed drug was huge!!

When I got over that initial shock, I walked to the nearest rubbish bin, disposed of this massive jar of some drug together with the repeat prescription, telling myself whilst in this state of anger that "There must be a better way, I am too young to be crippled with this disease!" Now many would have just accepted this 'specialist' doctor's advice and travelled on down that road of pain, despair and a crippled body before an inevitable shortened life. Why did I not accept that reality?

Answer: **Because it was not part of God's Plan for me,** that's why! Did I know what God's Plan was for me from that day forward? Of course not! But something, God's messages perhaps, encouraged me to go on and do extensive personal research on my health issues resulting in me changing my diet, increasing my daily exercise, changing how I lived, praying, visiting health resorts, practising daily meditation, 'letting go' of anger, experiencing time out and much, much more. I distinctly remember telling myself at that time that I would forsake any material wealth that I had currently accrued, spend whatever I had to and go to wherever I had to go to find a cure for my ailments. Why did I choose this course and not that of the 'specialist' doctor's plan for me? Answer: because it was **God's Plan** for me to take this course! Did I know that at the time? No, of course not! But I now know that it was NOT in **God's Plan** for me to follow the advice of this doctor or any other doctor at that time.

Over the many years that have followed that period in my life, I have often wondered about the next patient who went into that 'specialist' doctor's room after I had come out, and how that young girl's life played out. I have no doubt if she received advice like that which I received then she would have had a very short and painful life indeed. And maybe **God's Plan** for this young girl was so that you and I would learn lessons from her short life, so the rest of us look after that precious gift that God/Spirit/Source/? has given us, which is that of life itself!

The very first 'precious gift' that we must express thanks and gratitude for <u>**daily,**</u> is that we are alive and breathing. If you ever wake one morning and think that you have nothing to be grateful for, just check your pulse! There is no doubt someone, somewhere in the world, will be far worse off at the start of their day than you are at the start of yours (e.g. refer to picture at front of the book). We must always strive to make the very most of this precious gift that we are given i.e. the gift of time. Great joy comes to those who learn the importance of **daily** counting their blessings for being alive, giving thanks and then making the very best of the incredible gifts that this life brings. Life itself is a gift of inestimable value! Begin the practice of being grateful for YOUR life and make it a <u>**daily habit!**</u>

Other examples of 'gifts' that we in rich Western societies so often easily take for granted include gifts as simple as the gift of breathing freely, the gift of our physical movement and good health, the gifts of being able to see, speak and hear clearly, our personal freedoms, our family, our job or

Be Grateful and Know that God has Your Master Plan

business, our home, the capacity to buy and the variety of foods that we have available to us, the gift of a plentiful supply of clean, running hot and cold water to bath in or to drink at the turn of a tap, electric power at the flick of a switch, etc. These are just a few examples of the countless 'gifts' that we receive in our lives every day, most of which we simply accept as an every day given! Be aware that there are literally billions of people in this World who are not so blessed as to have something as basic as electric power or clean running water available to them at the flick of a switch or turn of a tap. **Think about that!**

So many of us spend so little of our time each day being Grateful for such 'gifts', as we tend to focus more on being 'busy', on 'doing', which is what makes us deceptively feel worthwhile and successful when we are already worthwhile just for being! Surely, each of us can find 15-20 minutes **daily**, preferably first thing in the morning, to focus on that which we have to be grateful for, starting with the fact that we have a pulse, that we are alive, breathing and moving! Being grateful and thankful for the small common things in our everyday lives is the first step on the path to a happy, peaceful, joyful and contented life. Living this way, we then live without fear and it is the absence of fear that creates this freedom and contentment!

What small things are YOU taking for granted in your life today? Maybe it's your vibrant physical and mental health, or the fact that you have a job that you love and earn a good income from, or is it a business that you own and operate, or the part of the world in which you live, or the home in which you live, or the partner that you have in your life, or your healthy, happy children and/or grandchildren, or whatever it might be. Just **STOP, PAUSE, REFLECT** for a few minutes right now and think about this. Stop and Think. And then focus on the sub-heading for this book: *Change Your Thinking = Change Your Life.*

You know, so many of us are afraid to think about, let alone talk about, death. Death does not need to be, nor should it be, a scary topic. Death is a reality! We all know that to be true and it is one thing that we all have in common. We will all die at some point! That is why we should all regularly pause and think about the inevitability of our death, be aware and grateful for our life, for the life of others and for the freedom that we have minute by minute to make conscious choices about what we think, say and do. Do not simply take your life for granted. Thinking about one's death encourages one to appreciate the present moment and to be continuously *Grateful and Thankful* for all that one has in their life. However, as expressed earlier, many people tend to focus on what they don't have rather than on what they do have. Or worse still, they focus on what someone else has and they don't. Continued personal suffering is the inevitable result of such thinking.

Once we adopt this **daily habit** of being consciously and continuously grateful and moving forward one step at a time, then old habits and negative long-held belief systems are slowly exposed and will ultimately fade away. We do however need to be gentle and forgiving with one's Self as this is a life changing process, and hence things will not change immediately. But if we commit to the habits outlined in this book, then a positive shift/change will happen. A dear friend, Arthur West, who passed away a few years back, would often recite the following piece to me, a quote which is still very much applicable for us all in the present day.

> 'It's plugging away that will win you the day
> So don't be a piker old pard.
> Just call on your grit, it's easy to quit.
> It's keeping on going that's hard.' – (Arthur West)

DAILY embrace that quote, embrace your life

Be Grateful.

Trust.

Be Patient.

Be Joyful.

Be Truthful

Be Courageous.

Be Alive!

Be YOU!

'Whatsoever you can do or dream you can, begin it. Boldness has genius, power and magic in it.' – (Johann Wolfgang von Goethe)

'Wisdom arises through effort and it disappears through lack of effort.' – Buddha

STOP, PAUSE, REFLECT here right now (the present moment) for a few minutes on the messages that you have received in this chapter.

I CAN NEVER BE NEGATIVE
IF I AM ALWAYS GRATEFUL!

Chapter 4:
Lack of Awareness

'The greatest Weakness in life is lack of Awareness.'
– (Buddha)

I came across this Buddhist quote some years ago that was a massive reality check for me, a **'light bulb'** moment if you like, the instant that I read it. A stark universal truth in just a few simple but powerful words! This statement is profound and incredibly powerful indeed when one takes the time to **STOP** and to think deeply on what it means! But sadly, many will not take that time to think deeply on this universal truth, and that is why they will never become **aware** that they lack this spiritual **awareness,** because no one has ever explained this concept to them. Developing **spiritual awareness** requires, among other things, openness, honesty, time, energy, patience, focus and commitment. We must ultimately come to realise and accept that

awareness is all that we should be seeking from life.

We must accept that we may need to think about and change our conscious thoughts/beliefs and be open to receiving new messages. However, as stated earlier, many limit themselves by adopting and maintaining a 'closed mind' approach to life. **Awareness** is the very first step along the path of transformation and change. To accept that we have travelled our life journey thus far searching for truth and understanding is the important first step on the pathway to becoming **aware,** and thus raising one's level of consciousness to a higher level.

Daily, one needs to stop all the 'noise' (i.e. social media and all other media platforms, work-related matters, home life issues, etc.) from the outside world, find a place to sit quietly in silence, preferably in or about nature, and begin the practice of **Looking Within.** By incorporating this **daily habit** into your life, over time, you can and will develop this essential life skill. It requires no more than simply just sitting quietly in solitude and thinking about what you are reading right now and about what's important in life.

Celebrate your achievements so far and be proud of your efforts to-date. However, do not beat yourself up or be hard on yourself. Be **aware** that you are not alone in life. Reach out to God/Spirit/Source/? for any help that you feel that you may need. You must first Ask, before you can Receive!

STOP, PAUSE, REFLECT. Take a few minutes right now to think deeply on this universal truth that *'The greatest Weakness in life is lack of Awareness.'*

Becoming **aware** does not mean that you must blame someone for where you are at in your life right now. Remember that our parents and family members were all very likely doing the best that they could, based on what they knew at the time. It is also probable that they would have done everything for you from a place of love and acted always in your best interests. Furthermore, remember that they learnt from their parents, who had learnt from their parents and so on. As stated earlier, they almost certainly just followed 'beliefs' imposed on them which had simply been passed down from generation to generation. Our beliefs determine who we are and our existence. Whatever you believe is what manifests in your life. Awareness really is just another term for 'wisdom'.

When you become wise, you respect your body, you respect your mind, you respect others, you respect your soul, and you respect YOU! Your life is then controlled by your heart and not by your head. Every day you have a chance to start over. You are reborn. You are brand new! You have received a gift, the 'precious gift' of life itself. You have another opportunity to change the things that you don't like in your life, a chance to improve your attitude to life, a chance to become **aware** and to work towards who you want to be. Be assured, my friend, that from this very moment on, each day of your life is a blank page in the book or movie titled: **'Your Life'.**

The pages up to this point in time in the book/movie: Your Life, can never be rewritten or altered in any way. However, YOU can write the next pages or movie scenes as YOU want your life to be. YOU are the sole author of the book or the director of the movie **'Your Life'.**

The question for you then becomes: How do you want these pages to read or the movie to run? YOU are in total control of that. YOU have your hands on the steering wheel of Your Life. If you choose to allow others to continue to turn that steering wheel for you then you obviously are not in total control of your life! You do however have the freedom to choose. It may not necessarily be easy, but you do have that freedom!

Sadly, for many, this is the exact point where they will choose to journey through the remainder of their life living in the dark, spiritually that is. They will continue unaware that they could live in a space of light (love). They will never experience the moment when they realise that step by step, they could become **aware!** They will continue to allow others to dictate what is written on the blank pages of the book of their life or to write the movie script of their life. Many will continue to live their lives in the dark, at least on a Soul level, rather than having the courage to deny this darkness and move to experience the joy and bliss of living life in a world of light (love). They will not live a life in Spirit, overseeing their own destiny while keeping their hands on the steering wheel of their life and directing where it goes. Choose right now to live YOUR life in the world of light (love).

Living in the free world, we are blessed to have the capacity to freely make thousands of choices every day, and we do, either consciously or subconsciously. Therefore, you can choose to live abundantly in a world of light/love and appreciate all the blessings that are available to you. Make it a **daily habit** to live this way, to **Look Within** and appreciate blessings like being able to breathe and move freely, speak, hear and see clearly, etc. Blessings that many of us take for granted **daily** as expressed earlier. It is only when we **STOP, PAUSE, REFLECT** and calm the mind that we begin to become aware of this fact.

So please, **STOP, PAUSE, REFLECT**. Feel free to put the book down right at this moment for a few minutes while you reflect deeply on what you have just read so far in this chapter. Take a few deep breaths to find a sense of calm, and then reflect again on the vitally important quote outlined at the start of this chapter and which is repeated below in large bold print.

Recite it to yourself until you too accept it as an '**awakening** moment/a light-bulb moment' in YOUR precious life. Have the courage to work through all your fears, make the shift and allow gentle change to flow. Become **aware** that whatever we 'believe' rules our life. The belief systems we have lived with until now have boundaries and limitations. Becoming **aware** changes all of that.

Affirm: Breath IN peace. Breath OUT stress.

(Do it now. Repeat as often as necessary, anytime, anywhere.)

The greatest Weakness in life is lack of *Awareness!*

Only when time in our outer world is balanced with time in our inner world will we move from darkness to light and hence become more **aware** of who we are meant to be. Initially, even 15-20 minutes a day sitting somewhere in silence, focusing on that 'inner world', can and will in due course make a significant difference in your life. For without this significant **daily habit,** nothing can or will change. Remember that famous quote of Zig Ziggler: *'If you always do as you have always done, then you will always get what you have always got.'* Unless you change your **daily habits,** how you think and the way that you go about living each day, nothing will change. Why would it!

Lasting happiness, inner peace and contentment can only be found from **within** the Self (you), not from outside of your Self. Not through being with some other person, being in another place, having more material possessions, a better job/career, owning a business, having social status, etc. These may bring short-term joy, and they usually do. They may be nice to have in your life, and they usually are. But true and lasting happiness can only come from **within!** Until one reaches a point where they believe this truth 100% and have faith in this fact of life, then one cannot and will not have **lasting happiness, inner peace and contentment**—again with the emphasis here on lasting! This is a universal truth. Disbelieve it at your peril and continued suffering!

Most of us battle through life basically having out of body experiences. We are stumbling from happy moments, to anger, to order, back to happy, then to frazzled, back to joy, then to stressed or maybe even to depressed, back to happy and on and on it goes with the cycle starting all over again, and then again and again. Why? It is because we have never learnt or been made **aware** that lasting happiness, inner peace and contentment can only come from **within.** Nowhere else. And yes, it does require courage to become **aware,** to believe, to accept and to have faith in this universal truth.

And so, we must learn to go **within** and seek the wisdom and guidance of our authentic Self. This can be a long process for many, but if we want to learn how to develop this amazing power, we must first be willing to take a leap of faith and trust in the processes as outlined in this book. If we let fear of the outcome stop us from taking such a leap of faith and to trust that this is so, then our life may be safe and expedient, but it will also be thin and shallow. And remember as stated earlier, fear is nothing more than False Evidence Appearing Real **(F. E. A. R)**

Furthermore, remember that other universal truth that I referred to in Chapter 1: **'The Greatest Enemy in Life is the Self.'** Yes, that's right, we can be, and often are, our very own worst enemy. Hard to believe? **STOP, PAUSE, REFLECT** for a moment right now and think long and hard again on this statement. Just **STOP** reading, put the book down, and take a few minutes to reflect again on this vitally important point that you may well be the greatest enemy in YOUR life, just as I was in my life until I learnt this universal fact and believed 100% that it is true. You MUST be completely open and honest with yourself to accept this universal truth, that how and what you think of yourself is often your greatest enemy. Personal growth can be confronting and uncomfortable. If you cannot be open and 100% honest with yourself, then the only person that you are deceiving is YOU!

Being completely open and sincere with your 'Inner Self' can be one of your greatest personal challenges in life. It requires real courage, absolute honesty and trust. But should you find the necessary courage to participate in this process, the outcome (positive changes in your life) will be truly magical. Give up struggling and start trusting. Trust in the **awareness** that resides within YOU. Allow yourself to flow more and let go of all your hurried thoughts for to find 'inner peace' is one's ultimate destiny. You may accumulate many worldly possessions, achieve social status, etc. but if you do not also have inner peace and contentment then you are certainly not wealthy.

Be **aware** and accept that things come and go. Thoughts come and go. People come and go. Days come and go. The seasons come and go, and just as in nature, we must accept on a deep level that nothing, and that means nothing, remains the same forever. *Everyone you meet, both the wise and the foolish, has something to teach you.* We are all teachers. In everything that you do be **aware**, be gentle, be kind, be thoughtful, be compassionate, be loving, be reasonable and be generous to all—including to yourself. Be the authentic YOU, and always maintain a joyful disposition.

'Mastering others is strength. Mastering yourself is true Power.' - (Lao Tzu)

STOP, PAUSE, REFLECT again for a few minutes on what you have just read in this chapter before you proceed.

The only constant in life is change. The **daily** acceptance of this inevitability of constant change in your life will allow life itself to flow more naturally. And always remember, life itself is not permanent. We will all die at some point. All life dies! Plants, animals, insects, humans. Every living thing in this material world ultimately dies. This is just a universal truth. When you accept this unconditionally and think deeply on it on a regular basis, then you open yourself up to the joy of living each day being Grateful and Thankful for the present moment. For ultimately, that is all that any of us has, the *Present Moment*.

When we are in those moments of heightened **awareness,** being present brings with it that overwhelming sense of joy that can only come from **within.** At that very moment when one accepts that the past is history and that the future (five minutes time, tomorrow, a week, a year, ten years, twenty years, and so on) is a mystery that is not guaranteed or promised to anyone, at that very moment of acceptance of this fact on a deep level, it is like a "light bulb' being switched on in one's brain. An explosion of light shining on the 'Inner Self', **awakening** one to this life-changing moment of truth.

As I briefly wrote earlier, the subject of death terrifies most of us. But let's face it, we are ALL going to die. The only mystery is that we do not know when. For most of us, we do not get to choose how or when we are going to die, we only get to choose how we are going to live! And we live right now, in the present moment. It is crucial to regularly be mindful of death and to contemplate that you will not remain forever in this life. This **awareness** and the acceptance of the impermanence of all life is a central and crucial part of developing wisdom. When you understand and accept on a deep Soul level that everything changes, that nothing stays the same forever, then and only then will you have a far better understanding and acceptance of all events that happen in your life.

That is why you should use the subject of death as a tool for living, and to realise **(be aware)** that every day of living is a 'precious gift'! Cemeteries are full of people who should have taken more quality breaks from their work or business but didn't. They thought they were irreplaceable — wrong! They should have read and acted on the advice received from good books but didn't. They should have spent more quality time alone and in nature but didn't etc. **Look Within** and develop good habits likes those outlined in this book and that will ensure, to the best of your ability at least, that you have a long, healthy, worthwhile, fulfilled and contented life.

STOP, PAUSE, REFLECT for a few moments on this vital point.

I Know That No Matter How Much I Protest I Am Totally Responsible for Everything That Happens to Me in My Life.

Every Day of Living is a Precious Gift...

NEVER Take It for Granted!

Chapter 5:
'The Past' is OUR Greatest Life Lesson

'The Past is nothing more than the trail that I have left behind, what drives my life today is the energy that I generate in each of my present moments.'
– (Oscar Wilde)

STOP, PAUSE, REFLECT for a few minutes each day and reflect on this very thought. Make it a **daily habit!**

When YOU accept unconditionally the above affirmation as to how we should regard our past, you are then *empowered* to always move forward without disappointment, regret, blame or guilt. And remember, the past is what you thought, or did, as little as one second ago. Reading the page before this page is now in your past. The past cannot be changed. For example, you cannot unread the previous pages. It is just that: past! Anything that happened five minutes ago, an hour ago, yesterday, last week or last year, can never be changed. It happened, and it happened in what is now your past! It is part of *the trail that you have left behind!*

That simple act of reading the previous pages of this book can never be changed. You cannot unread them. What you can change, however, is how you think, speak and act from this point forward. A true life is lived when tiny changes are made, one small step at a time, one day at a time. Just work along with this excellent quote: inch by inch it's a cinch.

Affirm:

'I cannot control the next chapter of my life if I keep re-reading the last chapter.' (Anonymous).

I want to share with you a life-changing experience that I had many years ago. This is a practical example of the power that comes from *'letting go'* of the past. Back at that time, I was a bachelor who happened to be going through a rather stressful and emotional break-up from a lady with whom I had been in a relationship with for some years. I was struggling emotionally, and I was beginning to doubt the person that I was, what I believed in, what my values were, what life was about, etc.

Ironically, while all of this was happening, I discovered the quote written at the start of this chapter in a book that I happened to be reading at the time. Reading the quote, I realised (became **aware**) that I was being somewhat too hard on myself. Rather than allowing these foreign emotions that I was experiencing to slip me into a state of what we now all too easily refer to as depression, I fortunately also discovered this next quote from Oscar Wilde. This next quote empowered me to 'Look Inward', encouraging me to believe and to accept that I was a good person. I subsequently formed an **awareness** that just because the relationship with this lady had not worked out, it did not automatically follow that I was lacking in any way or that either of us was at fault.

I copied this next powerful quote onto sticky notes and placed them on my bathroom mirror, my wardrobe door, the refrigerator door, the pantry door, on the outside of the shower screen, over the kitchen sink, on my car dashboard, etc. so that I would frequently see it and read it until I 100% believed what it said. This ultimately led to it becoming a core belief in my *belief system*. To this day, this next quote was, and still is, an incredible source of inner strength and power for me if or when required. I urge you to choose to make it a part of your authentic 'belief system' too, for when you truly understand, accept and adopt this simple

'The Past' is OUR Greatest Life Lesson

quote into your daily life, it will empower you also! Write it down and never forget it. The quote is one which you have already read back in Chapter 2 and which I repeat here: **'It matters little what others say and think of me, it matters much what I say and think of myself.'**

When you **STOP, PAUSE, REFLECT** and meditate on this quote and accept and trust it to be 100% true, then you too will discover it to be an extremely powerful force in YOUR life. Because at the end of the day, it does not matter what others say or think of you, what matters most in YOUR life is what YOU say and think of yourself! Too many of us struggle <u>daily</u> with worrying about what others may be saying or thinking about us, and such an approach to life can be, and is, incredibly destructive.

We live with ourselves 24/7, 365 days of each year, and the constant chatter of that little voice in our head (our Ego) is what we must learn to control. The first step in learning how to tame, dissolve or control that little voice (our Ego) is to tell it that what you say and think of yourself is all that matters. You will begin to experience an exciting **awakening** in your life as you gradually become **aware** of how your Ego has had such a controlling influence in your life up to this point.

Choose to be selective with your battles and you will slowly but surely discover that sometimes peace of mind is better than being right. One way to assist that thought process is to accept that there is no right or wrong, there just IS. Being angry and overthinking is not worth the energy. One must learn to let things go, remain positive and to be grateful, particularly grateful for having a pulse!

As you move forward from here one small step (change) at a time, old habits and thoughts about whether you are good enough will begin to lose their strength. Remember, it is your life journey, no one else can walk it for you. Other well-intentioned people (including myself) may offer you help/advice, but no one can live your life for you, no matter who you are or where you live. Your life is your very own 'precious gift', and you are the one in charge and responsible for it!

When you are consciously and consistently trying to be the very best that you can be (i.e. your authentic Self), you will slowly experience magic in this life-changing process. A shift will happen! You must just allow time, be open, be honest, be disciplined, stay focused, commit to the process and be willing to embrace the positively magical changes that will eventuate. It is vital that you are patient with the process and gentle with yourself.

Patience is simply the calm acceptance that things may happen in a different timeframe than that which you may have had in mind.

'Patience is surrendering to the present and allowing destiny to unfold at its own pace.' – (Nari)

'To the mind that is still, the whole universe surrenders.' – Lao Tzu

Remember that you are not trying to achieve anything in a physical sense, but rather, you are merely seeking to change how you think. As always though, beware the Ego (much more on the Ego in the next chapter). Have faith in the process/path that you are following here. And to have faith is to be 100% without doubt. Know that faith comes from the heart not from the head, from love not fear. Faith is our personal power. Furthermore, be **aware** that if you say that you cannot do something, then guess what? It naturally follows that you can't! For that reason, try to never use the word 'can't' in whatever you say!

Without faith in a Higher Power (e.g. God/Source/Spirit/?) then you will travel through life like a ship without a rudder, bouncing from one life obstacle/drama to another, to another, to another, and so on. When one has learnt the importance of connecting **daily** with that Higher Power, then one tends to sail through life on much calmer waters. There is less turbulence. Obstacles/dramas will still appear from time to time, but with that 'inner spiritual light' shining brightly, and belief and faith that you are working with a Higher Power, then you will be able to navigate such matters in a calmer more controlled manner.

We may not be able to control all the events that happen in our life, but with faith in a Higher Power and a **daily** connection with that Higher Power, one can then control their attitude to any such turbulence in a more controlled way. However, if you choose to remain in a state of unconsciousness and stay asleep at the steering wheel of your life, then authentic <u>**lasting**</u> **happiness, inner peace and contentment** will continually prove elusive. Reward requires, and always follows, effort. In addition, with this process of learning the importance of **Looking Within,** it requires you to focus and to make a long-term commitment to do the 'inner work' that is vital for successful outcomes.

It Matters Little What Others Say and Think of Me, It Matters Much What I Say and Think of Myself!

The changes that WILL follow this 'Inner Work' that you will undertake here, I refer to as **'light bulb moments'**. When you experience for the first time the magic of positive change in your deep, inner thoughts, it is like a 'light bulb' suddenly being turned on in your brain and in your heart! There is an explosion of light/thought when suddenly you become **aware** for the very first time of something magical that you have just discovered about life! About yourself! It's an incredibly powerful moment of truth. At this very point, each small step is an achievement. Be proud that you have made the effort. It is my hope for YOU that you experience many *'light bulb'* moments the entire time that you are working with this book.

Remember that story of the man who complained because he had no shoes? That was until he saw a man who had no feet! Make it a **daily habit** to be grateful and thankful for all that you have in your life. Learn to distinguish between needs and wants. We 'need' food to survive, but to 'want' a bigger house, a better motor vehicle, a better job, etc. is not essential or a prerequisite to manifesting **lasting happiness, inner peace and contentment**.

Pray **daily** for guidance with this powerful transformation process that you will now be engaged in as God/Spirit/Source/? asks for nothing more. Neither should you. Good things will happen in their time. All that is required of you is to fully participate, remain focused, and to be patient (i.e. calm acceptance that things will happen when they are meant to). Simply have faith and trust that the 'magic' will follow. Give up the need to know why things happen as they do and begin to accept things as they are! This is wisdom. And remember, wisdom arises through effort. Regardless of your age or your past, simply be open to this new approach to life, to a new beginning. Allow your thinking to 'stretch' and envelop these new circumstances. Be Brave! Be Bold! Be **Aware!** *BEGIN!*

Affirm: Surrender to what is. - **The Present.**

Let go of what was. - **The Past.**

Have faith in what will be. - **The Future.**

Give up the Need to Know Why Things Happen as They do and Begin to Accept Things as They Are! This is Wisdom.

Being Present and Grateful

*'I choose to live my life in the Present Moment and appreciate each day for what it is —
a PRECIOUS GIFT.'*
– (Dr Wayne Dyer)

When we choose the joy of living our lives in the 'present moment', we suddenly realise (**'light bulb moment'**) that we generally have everything that we need in life to make us happy, but we have simply lacked the conscious **awareness** it takes to appreciate this fact. (<u>Remember</u>: *'the greatest enemy in life is the Self'* as described earlier.) When we do take the time each day to **STOP, PAUSE, REFLECT** and acknowledge all the good that already exists in our lives, we can then offer the Universe the gift of our grateful heart. Simple pleasures are often overlooked, so grasp the **awareness** of what it is that truly makes you happy.

It may be something as simple as waking after a restful and peaceful night's sleep in a warm, comfortable bed, or owning your own home debt free, or being **aware** that you have enough money every day to provide for yourself and/or your family. Or it may be as simple as living in a quiet, safe environment, free from the nightmare of living with war and its associated chaos for example. Or being able to hug your child daily, or simply having a healthy mind and body. Maybe it is building a successful online or traditional business.

Maybe it is writing a book like this one to help others to become **aware** of what really matters in life! Or being able to walk or jog on a beach or on a bush track. Or having a very special partner in your life. Or being able to go for a swim or a surf each day. Or maybe it's as simple as just being able to help a friend or a stranger with something that they need to do, or to enjoy cooking and sharing a meal. Or playing a musical instrument. Maybe it's as simple as playing with your own healthy, happy child or grandchild or doing volunteer work, etc. The list is limitless and different for each of us.

Happiness is a State of Mind. Happiness is always a choice! Nothing can make you happy until you 'choose' to be happy! Happiness cannot come to you, it can only come from **within** YOU! It comes from how you perceive things, the quality of your thoughts and your Beliefs. Happiness is a living emotion. The magic seeds of happiness and contentment are planted deep **within** each of us. Genuine and lasting happiness can only be realised once we commit to making it a personal priority in our life. And that is why it can only come from **within!** True lasting happiness is not a possession. It cannot be bought.

STOP, PAUSE, REFLECT right now on what you have in YOUR life today, to be grateful for. Start with the fact that you have a pulse! Make a list as you will need it after reading the remainder of this book.

Affirm: 'I am living in the present moment and I am truly grateful.'

For Christmas 2013, my wonderful wife Liz gave me what ultimately was the most useful and satisfying material 'gift' that I have ever received. However, I was not immediately **aware** of that at the time. The 'gift' was a book known as a **Gratitude Journal,** and until that moment in time, I couldn't remember ever even having heard of such a thing as a **Gratitude Journal.**

Despite this, from that day forward, I rapidly became **aware** of the importance of writing in such a Journal **daily** the many things that I am grateful for, and the power that this simple action has for one's grasp of what matters in one's life. This truly is a life-changing practice when adopted and practised **daily!** One quickly appreciates so many things that are important to sustaining a happy and healthy life, many of which we generally just take for granted!

I would never have believed that writing in such a Journal at least **five** things every day, could create such inner peace, personal power, **awareness** and growth. Should you decide to acquire your own

Gratitude Journal (*I highly recommend that you do*) and develop the **daily habit** of writing in it, you too will be amazed at how the simple practice of writing in a Journal can have such a profound and positive effect on your life.

Trust me, because it may be the most rewarding small investment that you make in your ongoing personal and spiritual development as it is for me. Let me give just one small example of what we all regularly take for granted in our daily lives. This is the very first point that I write in my **Gratitude Journal daily**.

'I am Grateful and Thankful that we have ALL awakened again today, still Breathing and Moving freely. We can still See, Speak and Hear clearly, Touch and Feel… Thank You, Thank You, Thank You.'

When I am writing the word 'We', I am thinking of those whom I love and care about, including myself! I always start my sentence with these two words: **I AM**. It is generally not until we have lost capacity in some way with any of the above 'gifts', that we suddenly become consciously **aware** of how precious such gifts are to our everyday life! We simply take them for granted, **daily!**

As you re-read this information on the **Gratitude Journal,** just take a few minutes to **STOP, PAUSE, REFLECT** and honestly think about this for it is possible that you, just like me, had until this very moment taken for granted everyday gifts as simple as those mentioned above. It is **vital** that we are open and brutally honest with ourselves about this! Breathing and Moving freely, being able to See, Speak and Hear clearly are precious 'gifts' that you too may have taken for granted until now when you have suddenly been made **aware,** are they not? Please, you *must* be open and honest with yourself as you answer this question!

There are many, many examples of simple experiences/gifts that we enjoy in our lives every day that many of us simply take for granted. Maybe it is a job that you love or a successful business that you own and operate. Maybe it's having a healthy mind and body, or a life partner that you love. Maybe it's being drug- free, or its the beautiful home that you live in, or maybe it's your happy, healthy children or grandchildren if you have them in your life, etc. Should one not pause each morning for a just few minutes and give **Thanks** for such blessings?

The moral of this message: *Do not take anything in your life for granted.* We must learn to practise **DAILY** being grateful for all that we have now, all that we have had in the past (both the good and the bad) and all that we may have in the future. Please, make this practice a **daily habit** in YOUR life. You will not regret it!

Ask yourself each morning: **"Today is my 'special gift' from God/Spirit/Source/? how will I use it?"**

Other examples of taking things for granted may include the fact that we, in most Western Countries at least, enjoy the freedom to make minute by minute choices about how we live our life. We have access to electric power at the flick of a switch, enjoy clean running water at the press of a button (toilet flush) or at the turn of a tap to drink or bathe in. We have choices as to the varieties of foods at a supermarket or farmer's market that we can choose from to nourish our body, as to the farmers who grow our foods, as to the truck drivers who deliver it to the stores, as to the packers who pack the supermarket shelves, as to our police and fireman, as to the school teachers, as to the authors of good books, and the list goes on and on.

Should one not simply **STOP, PAUSE, REFLECT** from time to time to whisper **Thank You,** or to write it in a Gratitude Journal! Maybe it's as simple as living in a Country free from the ravages of war and conflict. Just taking a walk through a spinal ward or the children's cancer ward of your local hospital will help you realise and focus on how fortunate YOU are. Be grateful for all our doctors and nurses who care for us when required, to our family members and others who love us, etc. The list is inexhaustible!

Again, **STOP, PAUSE, REFLECT** right now and take another look at that picture at the front of this book, think about and be grateful for all that you have in YOUR life right now! When you purchase your own **Gratitude Journal** you will slowly but surely build a list of matters that are personal to you and that you will want to write into that Journal **daily.** Writing **five things** that you are personally grateful for every day into such a journal truly is a brilliant way of expressing Gratitude. It is just a matter of doing it until it becomes a **daily habit!**

I have mentioned this practice to friends from time to time and unfortunately, the response is "Yes, I am grateful for all of that, **but** I don't have time to write it in a Journal." There's the ego at work. Unfortunately, this is an all too common response and this is from the very same people who regularly struggle with a variety of issues in their lives and who possibly will never discover the true pathway to **lasting happiness, inner peace and contentment.** i.e. thinking **daily** about how much you have to be Grateful for, and then adding those two extremely powerful words: **Thank You!**

A happy and contented life really is that simple! It's not rocket science, but rather, nothing more than learning to live in the 'present moment' and to be grateful! The daily **Gratitude Journal** writing MUST become a ritual, a **daily habit**, just like getting out of bed. It MUST become a part of your everyday living, something that you do automatically, for it has now become part of who YOU are. No other person or a digital machine of some description can do this **daily** exercise for you. Inner joy and empowerment come from the physical act of writing in that journal!

STOP, PAUSE, REFLECT on the **Gratitude Journal** process.

This is a vitally important Chapter!

I Choose to Live My Life in The Present Moment and Appreciate Each Day for What It Is — *A PRECIOUS GIFT!*

Chapter 6:
The Ego and its Problems— Learn to 'Let Go'

'The Greatest Enemy in Life is the Self'
– (Buddha)

Magic begins to happen when you become **aware** for the very first time that what is important in YOUR life is what YOU say and think of yourself. Maybe when this concept is believed, is fully accepted and enacted in your life, it will be a powerful 'light bulb' moment for you as it was for me. Simply **STOP, PAUSE, REFLECT,** surrender to it and allow the experience you feel having read again the following Buddha quote: **The Greatest Enemy in Life is the Self.** And the Ego is the Self! Many, when they read or hear this universal fact of life for the very first time, tend to resist or deny what they have just read or heard believing that they do not have an **Ego.**

The Ego and its Problems — Learn to 'Let Go'

Pride is sometimes a great inhibitor. But it is a fact, we ALL have an Ego.

Rather than resisting that which you may be feeling right now, just try to go with those feelings. Be flexible and 'let go' of the need for control. Let go of the need to be right. Let go of the need to know why. Let go of that sense of self-pride. Let go of the messenger (i.e. in this instance this author) and concentrate on the message. *Just Go with the Flow.* There is a rhythm to life, an ebb and flow. We give energy and we receive energy. And at the exact moment you realise this, your Ego will fight. The Ego is only interested in its own survival.

The Ego can be simply thought of as that voice in your head that chatters constantly from the time you wake each morning until you fall asleep again at night. It will fight to remain in control, and it will struggle with you to say no to all that is empowering you to change how you think or act in any given moment. The Ego may have had control of you for a very long time and so, it will fight to have you stay where you are in life. Your Ego does not want you to develop and grow on an emotional or spiritual level. *The Ego wants to present you to the world as you would like to be seen rather than who you really are.* This outer illusion of who you are and where you sit in the world is the major preoccupation of the Ego.

Look Within

The Ego creates limitations and manufactures problems that do not really exist, for example, that you are not good enough, you are not smart enough, you are not attractive enough, you are overweight, you are too short, you do not deserve certain things, etc. By learning to tame or dissolve your Ego, you then enable your higher level of **awareness**, or consciousness, to flow. For it is only then that you will become **aware** that you do not have to compete with or be better than anyone else. You no longer necessarily need to accumulate materially to achieve, or to seek more from your outer world to be accepted. You are perfect just as you are right now, in this present moment. Buddha once said that our spiritual task in life is to learn how to overcome the Ego, or at least learn how to control it.

When you become **aware** of your Ego and learn how to control or to dissolve it, you will then begin to experience life as being connected to all rather than separate from others. You will also discover that something outside of yourself cannot yield <u>**lasting happiness, inner peace and contentment**</u>. When you learn and accept the importance of turning your thoughts to your 'inner path', you will begin to realise and accept, maybe for the very first time, that we are all connected to God/Spirit/Source/? and to all of life.

You must realise and accept that it is impossible to consume your way to lasting happiness, inner peace and contentment, which is the opposite of what certain media is telling you. For example, you cannot purchase authentic love from a retail outlet or from an online store! When you learn to discontinue from seeking that which cannot be obtained from outside of yourself, you relax in peacefulness. You are learning to tame the Ego! You must, however, be **aware** that the Ego always loves to be right, and the Ego does not like change.

I will repeat that: *The Ego does NOT like change!* Subsequently, it will do it's very best to resist any positive changes that you may now try to make to how you think or act. The Ego wants to always be in control, and it thrives on fear and the approval of others. The Ego can be thought of as our 'social mask'. The mantra of the Ego is to have more, more, more: more money, more investments, more ownership, more clothes, better social status and image of Self, etc. and it always needs to be right.

This need for control, the need to be recognised, the need for approval, the need to be right and the need for external power (symbols of success) are all fear based. Therefore, when you allow yourself to **STOP, PAUSE, REFLECT** and to be completely open and honest with your 'Inner Self', accepting as truth that which you are discovering in the pages of this book, then a 'shift' in your thinking will subtly manifest. When you are being totally honest with yourself, you cannot lie to your heart. You cannot deceive your authentic Self. Short-term, you can fool yourself, maybe, but you cannot sustain it long-term!

Social Masks

The Ego wants us to wear invisible social masks! An invisible mask or wall around us (an image of our self) designed to block out the real You, the authentic You, from being seen or heard. However, once you are **aware** of this fact, accept and acknowledge it to be true, then you can choose to shed these invisible masks and experience the freedom of showing the real You to your family, friends and to everyone you meet. This is the best and most perfect thing that one can do in their life — be their authentic Self.

Why should one shed their mask?

1. Because you will then bring all that you are to all that you do. Remember, there is no one just like you. You are unique. You are perfect just as God made you without the need for the self-imposed 'social masks' worn to impress others!

2. Putting on and taking off social masks is emotionally exhausting. Those who continue to wear their social masks long-term often turn to drugs, alcohol or other forms of self-abuse to cover the emotional pain of being masked. Worse, they start forgetting who they really are as behind the mask is their true Self, which they themselves will eventually fail to recognise. Think Actors. These people are a classic example of wearing a 'mask'. They spend weeks, possibly months or even years, 'role-playing' a scripted or fictional character, and the actor must learn to be that personality for hours, for days, weeks or months.

Subsequently, when one is doing that day, after day, after day for long periods of time, they may also be required to simultaneously 'role-play' a completely different fictional character in an alternate movie or TV mini-series of some description during that very same period. As a result, because of all these invisible masks that they wear at various times, the actor may ultimately begin to struggle with remembering who they really are. They forget their authentic Self.

Hence, it is because of these invisible 'masks' (changed personalities) that they must wear that so many in that industry have problems with drug and alcohol abuse, failed relationships, depression, suicide, sexual misconduct issues, etc. And so, it can be the same for the rest of us. If we try to portray our self as someone other than who we really are (our authentic Self) then, over time, we can and will have similar problems. If we project a false image (social mask) of our self to others in our space, whether that be in our work or social environment, then we are potentially doomed to have similar emotional issues at some point. That is why you should not dress to impress others, but rather, dress to impress yourself. Let go of feeling the need to impress or please others, unless you are fully aware that this is what you are doing by choice!

3. Masks make you **shallow and thin** where God/Spirit/Source/? intended you to be **deep and rich.** Everything and everyone in our lives gets cheated when we choose to hide our true Self behind invisible 'social masks'. We were not born with masks, we put them on. Therefore, we can choose and take them off. Think about the mask(s) that **YOU** may be wearing and take them off. Be authentic. Be the true You! Why are we so afraid to be authentic and just be our true Self? No one is perfect. Life is life and it will never be perfect. Asking or seeking help takes courage, it is not a weakness. Open yourself up emotionally, live mask-free and allow love and support to flow to you. If you want people to love you for who you are, take off the masks and be free! One cannot have healthy, lasting relationships or friendships with people who wear masks. Ditch your masks and let others in. Your life will then be rich and deep, not thin and shallow.

'I am always free to Let Go and observe My Life"
– (Unknown)

When we shed the masks, we enjoy the freedom of just being who we really are, just as God wanted us to be, our authentic true Self. No more pretending. You give others a chance to share in the authentic You. *Wearing 'social masks' isolates you from good people.* Masks are a sign of weakness and are harming you by creating resistance to you being your natural Self. We can choose to live in denial, but ultimately, ill health, disease, drug abuse, relationship failures, depression, excessive alcohol consumption or other unwanted outcomes will materialise. You must honestly ask yourself: Do your family and friends love/like you, or is it the mask(s) that you wear that they love/like?

Don't hang out with those who don't help you to shine, but rather, spend most of your time in the company of those who nourish and inspire you. Be with those that feed your flame, believe in you and support you. The people whom you currently spend most of your time with, honestly ask yourself, are they going to help make or break your dreams? And remember that which you read earlier, **you are the average of the five people with whom you spend most of your time!**

STOP, PAUSE, REFLECT honestly now for a few minutes on this principle of 'social masks' before continuing your reading.

With a positive 'shift' in your level of **awareness/** consciousness you will by now have not only become **aware** that the Ego is resisting (notice your feelings right now), but you will begin to smile, realising that you have learnt maybe for the very first time, how it is possible for you to now control or dissolve your Ego, rather than the Ego controlling you! No doubt there have been times in our life that we can all recall that we have had the need or desire to be right. This is the Ego creating the illusion of problems where there really aren't any. That is how Ego works. It reminds me of the old saying from Mark Twain as he came closer to his death: **'I'm an old man, I had many problems, but most of them didn't happen. I spent much of my life worrying about things that never happened.'** No doubt we can all relate to that statement.

As I wrote earlier, Buddha believed that the greatest single challenge we will have in our life is learning how to control our Ego (the Self). When we become **aware** of this fact, accept it to be true and master how to control or dissolve it, for then magic happens! Persist with it, and that 'shift' *WILL* happen in your life too. It is a gradual shift, but it does come with enormous benefits. Participate fully, be consistent, stay focused, be brutally honest with yourself, be grateful for the small steps, be gentle with yourself, be patient and YOU WILL WIN! Abandon your Ego, that which identifies you with the world of achievement, possessions and being better than others!

'When your heart is open and truthful, the Ego will melt like snow does when exposed to the sun.'
– (Unknown)

STOP, PAUSE, REFLECT here for a few minutes. Re-read if need be to fully understand this Chapter thus far because it is *vital* that you understand and accept this life-changing message.

Sadly though, from my experience, it is at this very point that many will turn-off the **'light bulbs'** (revelations), preferring to remain in the 'darkness' with their Ego in control. Why? Because this is the easier option. For it is the light, not the dark (the Ego), that frightens us. The dark, with the Ego in control, is where we can feel comfortable and stable. In Australia we have a small bug know as a cockroach which can grow up to some 1-2 inches in length and likes to live inside people's homes. If at night you turn on a light in your home and there is a cockroach in that room, it will quickly scamper away and disappear to somewhere dark. Why? Because it feels safe in the dark. Humans often choose to live like this too, in that they choose to live their life in the dark. In spiritual darkness or spiritual denial.

Hence, those who choose to live in this spiritual darkness are like the cockroach in that they feel safe living in spiritual darkness. Why? Because it is what they are used to, what they have been 'conditioned' to do from a young age as explained earlier. It is easier, it's where they feel safe and comfortable and so, the Ego subsequently remains in control. These individuals, like the Ego, do not like change. *Do not be one of them!* It is in the world of Spiritual light (Love) that we see opportunities for change, and it is the thought of this change that can scare us (our Ego) and others in our 'environment', because change can be challenging and uncomfortable. Remember what I wrote earlier, that the Ego does NOT like change. Living in spirit/light exposes this fear. And that is why one needs to remember that 'fear' may stand for nothing more than **f**alse **e**vidence **a**ppearing **r**eal **(F.E.A.R)**.

It does not matter the circumstances, whether it be in your business, your career, a relationship or whatever it might be, just know and accept that it is okay to fail. We all experience failures in our lives, from the leaders of corporations or countries to ordinary unassuming but unique people just like you and I. Everybody experiences failure at some point. But it is having courage that ultimately defines us, as we continue to pursue our dreams. And that is what authentic living is all about. Pursuing **YOUR** dreams with integrity and courage! Failures are just small stumbles or bumps on the road to success.

As I have just said, many will feel more comfortable remaining in that 'spiritual darkness' of the Ego living with what they currently know, feeling safe and secure, because change, as I also said, can be a confronting and uncomfortable process. Change requires us to be 100% honest with our Self, and to 'stretch' on an emotional level. Unfortunately, many are not prepared to do this because when confronted with this scenario, they simply fear change. We may want change but are just unable to take that leap of faith required to burst into the magical place of Light. As always, throughout this process, it is vital that one be brutally honest with one's Self.

I know that I am strengthened as I seek to make truth my personal reality.

Remember again that famous Zig Ziglar quote that I wrote earlier: *'If you always do as you have always done then you will always get what you have always got.'* In other words, if you keep living your life doing and thinking the same way then nothing will change. Why would it? And this is the big challenge, to openly and honestly, learn the skill of **Looking Within** and practising it <u>daily</u>. I urge you to put the book down right now and to slowly recite this Zig Ziglar quote to yourself three or four times, at least, before you read on. One needs to recite this exact quote to themselves on numerous occasions throughout their day over the coming days, weeks and months ahead. Do it until you accept unconditionally that if you do not change how you think and act then your life will simply not change.

And so, you must ask yourself, are you ready for change? Do you really want to change? If you answer yes to these two questions, then it will require *full participation, focus, patience and commitment* to the process. Should you do that, in time, magic will happen. And always: Do not give your energy to any who think that you cannot change, especially not to your Ego!

You must by now understand and accept why it is imperative to be open and completely honest with your Self, to not deceive your Self, and why it is always necessary to fight back against the Ego. It is why you MUST remain flexible, keep those **'light bulbs'** shining brightly (do not be a cockroach!) and always be open to and embrace positive change. Flexibility and being open to change bring with them pleasures and surprises that can only come about by not being rigid. It is critical that you are always open to learning and to constantly welcome change. Be **aware** that once change happens, you can never go back to the way you were.

When you acknowledge and accept the fact that YOU are the one responsible for everything in YOUR life, things will immediately be different for you. Improve your 'Inner Self' each day and you improve your life. Make it a habit, a **daily habit**, to repeat to yourself as many times in a day as you can: **I know that no matter how much I protest, I am totally responsible for everything that happens to me in my life.**

I do accept that there will be those who may struggle to accept this proposition, and in most instances, sadly, these will be the very same people who journey through their entire life always denying, defending, justifying, or blaming someone or something for all that happens to them on their life journey. More on this in Chapter 9. The acceptance of change on a deep Soul level, whatever that change might be, will allow your life to flow more freely. You MUST trust yourself with this concept. May you awaken to the magnificent light of your own true nature.

**I REALISE THAT
I AM ALWAYS FREE
TO 'LET GO' AND
OBSERVE MY LIFE!**

The Ego and its Problems — Learn to 'Let Go'

You are learning every day, and the reality is that You are precisely how you are meant to be at this point of time in your life. If you don't like how your life is right now, then let's do something to improve it. Maybe a good place to start is as simple as always choosing to take complete responsibility for ALL that you say and do, whilst striving to be the very best that you can be in all that you say and do. BELIEVE that you can improve your life, because ultimately only you can do that! No one else can do it for you. There may be times when you feel like giving up. We all need patience, focus, commitment, perseverance and support. Others can help, but only you can make it happen! Don't bully yourself though. Be kind to yourself first and foremost. You may just need to meet up and connect with others who share a similar vision.

Most stress in our lives results from holding onto those old 'beliefs' that keep us striving for more (i.e. more money, more houses, more cars, more clothes, more, more, more) because the Ego stubbornly believes we need it, and that having 'more' will result in us being happier. But you have now learnt to at least question that proposition!

At a seminar, a doctor once said, "The best medicine for all humans is Love."

Someone then asked, "But doctor, what if it doesn't work?"

The doctor simply smiled and replied, "Just increase the dose!"

When we make the emotional shift away from the 'attachment' to material possessions, the influence (power) of the Ego diminishes and we replace that emotional attachment with contentment. Seeking more and more and then becoming 'attached' to what we have sought, is the main source of anxiety and suffering in the world today. This incessant pursuit of having 'more' does not of its self, feed our needs on a Soul level. Buddhist's describe this practice as the **'Law of Attachment'** and they believe it is our single greatest cause of suffering. Having or acquiring material assets in our lives is not the problem, it is our attachment to them that causes the suffering — more on this later.

Our Ego is always prompting and prodding us to go after more and more of the material world's success symbols. More money, more properties, more social popularity, etc. but inside **(Within)** at the end of it all, materially successful people often have this constant gnawing feeling of 'is this all that there is to life?' When we continually follow Ego thinking, we ultimately feel unfulfilled on that deeper level, on a Soul level. Daring to fight the Ego and step out of its conformity always brings unanticipated rewards and pleasures. Develop the practise/**daily habit** of turning away from the rigors of the world for a few minutes each day to **STOP, PAUSE, REFLECT** and to *listen to those whispers of your heart and soul* as you deeply Look Within. Participate fully, focus, be patient, and MAGIC will happen!

Letting Go of the Attachment

I want to share with you a personal example of *believing and accepting* in the need and the benefits of being able to 'let go'. When my brother (Laurie) was in the final stages of his battle with cancer before his ultimate passing in January 2015, my two sisters, my wife Liz and myself, were confronted with some unfortunate incidents with my brother's wife and his adult children. I do not need to elaborate on the specifics other than to say that the circumstances were quite confronting during such an emotionally sad time and should never have happened. To come to terms with what happened at this extremely stressful time and then, longer term, to not allow such circumstances to have more permanent ramifications in my life and in the life of my wife Liz, I took the difficult decision to emotionally 'let go' of my sister-in-law and her adult children.

At the time, this was an exceedingly difficult decision to make, but once such a decision has been made in your head and in your heart, and you accept it 100% as the best way forward for yourself and for all those concerned, you are then prepared for whatever comes after that. In this instance, the process itself was relatively easy. I was able to verbalise and visualise myself forgiving these individuals for what had transpired, I forgave them all, wished them well for their futures and then simply *'let go'* and had no further contact.

Subsequently, there have been no long-term repercussions for having adopted this approach, in fact, it has been quite the opposite. For me personally and for my wife, I believe this decision has proven to be the best way forward for all concerned. Having mentally 'let go', my wife and I have had no further contact with either my sister-in-law or her adult children since that event.

Another powerful example of 'letting go' is the story Dr Wayne Dyer tells of a Buddhist monks' encounter in a busy airport lounge. The monk was sitting in the lotus position in the airport lounge doing silent meditation. A young man walking past, stopped and commenced berating the monk for sitting there like that in a public place wearing weird clothes and looking out into space. The monk simply ignored the young man and continued to meditate.

Eventually, the young man became somewhat bored with not being able to gain any reaction from the monk and so went on his way. A young couple who had been sitting nearby observing what had just taken place, approached the monk as he was packing up his things and inquired as to why he had just sat there and ignored the young man's obnoxious behaviour. The monk casually looked up at them and in a soft, gentle voice, replied, **"If someone offers you a gift and you choose not to accept it, to whom does the gift belong."** The monk, at that very point when the young man was yelling at him, just chose not to accept what the young man was offering (the verbal tirade), he just *'let it go'*. Subsequently, when the young man moved away, so did the problem!

A very good lesson for us all! When confronted with something, or by someone, that you do not want to accept, just let it go. And always remember that powerful and very appropriate saying: **'Let Go, Let God.'** This is so true! In this instance, the problem that the young man had, whatever that may have been, was between himself and God and had nothing to do with the monk, who simply chose not to buy into the young man and God's business. Letting Go is simple really, but in practice not necessarily easy!

Then, of course, Mother Nature gives us the great leveller on how to 'let go'. Think of all the trees that just naturally and without any fuss *'let go'* of their leaves every year, year after year! One can always learn a lot from just sitting and observing nature. *Letting go of your need to control will let you and others be free!*

**I REALISE THAT
I AM ALWAYS FREE
TO 'LET GO' AND
OBSERVE MY LIFE!**

Chapter 7:
My Daily Practice

'I know that in each moment I am free to decide.'
– (Author Unknown)

I now want to share with you a very important part of my morning practice, a **daily habit** which involves 'special prayers' and other material that I have been drawn to reciting **daily** for the last fifteen years plus. These have led to the **awareness** that I have this very strong calling/purpose/passion to share these daily habits so that you too can embrace the very same life-changing practices to enrich your life, as they have mine. Hence, this book: **Look Within.**

These prayers, which are merely a cluster of powerful sentences that I recite during my *'alone, quiet time'* every morning, are the prayers together with many affirmations that make me who I am. They have empowered me to become a self-confident, responsible, joyful, worthwhile, happy and contented person. If you make a commitment to take 15-20 minutes of your day (*approximately 1% of any 24-hour period*), preferably first thing every morning, to recite these same prayers and affirmations softly to yourself with passion and belief (*Habits* develop *Beliefs* and *Beliefs* develop *Behaviour*), then over time, this practise will result in positive changes subtly happening in your life too. Just believe, have faith, and trust in the process. Focus, commit to doing it each morning, be patient, be disciplined, and positive change will happen! Developing these daily habits is at the very core of this transformational process, together with being kind and patient with yourself and with the process.

Yes, I do believe in God/Spirit/Source/? however, I do not regard myself as being a 'religious person' in the traditional sense since I rarely attend any traditional church services. What I am sharing with you in this book is *not* about any specific religion. However, if you are a religious person, that's fine. If you are not religious but believe in God/Spirit/Source/Buddha/Allah/The-Angels/? or whatever YOU believe in, that's fine too.

Remember: **Habits** develop **Beliefs**. **Beliefs** develop changes in **Behaviour**. Therefore, it is that ritual, the repetition of doing this **daily** routine, that will ultimately reveal positive change in YOU!

Prayer is simply using certain powerful sentences to ASK God/Spirit/Source/? for your 'inner power' to be turned on. Think of it as turning on the electricity in your body. You are turning on the light/spirit in your life! You are leaving the darkness of the Ego and turning on the light of love in your heart. You are starting to listen to those *'whispers of your heart'* instead of to your head, and to the Ego. Your soul is becoming visible and known to you. This is *powerful energy* that you are unleashing! Where you read the word God, if you must, just substitute your own word. It is merely reference to that Higher Power that I discussed back in Chapter 5. Stay with me here and read on, as there is great 'inner power' in the words that we choose to use.

This is the first of my **'Morning Prayers'**. I will then follow on and explain the 'power' of these words after the full text of the prayer.

Dear God, Thank You for this new day, its Beauty and its Light.

Thank You for my Chance to Begin Again. Thank You, Thank You, Thank You

Free me, God, from the Limitations of Yesterday. Today may I be Reborn

May I become more fully a Reflection of Your Radiance

Dear God, give me Strength, Compassion, Courage and Wisdom

Show me the Love in Myself and in Others

May I recognise the Good that is available Everywhere

May I be, this day God, an Instrument of Love and Healing

Lead Me into Gentle Pastures and

Give Me Deep Peace God so that I might Serve You Most Deeply

Almighty God and Guardian Angels I give You Thanks and Praise

Amen.   (Marianne Williamson)

I will now break down each line of this prayer and as YOU begin to slowly and 'softly whisper' each of the prayers to yourself, day after day, you too will feel the 'power' that these words have. Words have amazing power if you think deeply on them as you slowly recite them. If you commit to reciting these prayers and affirmations **DAILY** (and I sincerely hope that you will) with *'passion and belief'* and are disciplined whilst trusting in them to be the Truth then, over time, the empowerment that you will experience can and will be remarkable as it has been for myself. We are all born equal. However, many of us have simply lost our way due to that 'conditioning' by our peers as I have discussed earlier in the book. Simply learn to seek spiritual guidance in dealing with your conflicts and challenges, and we all have those!

As I mentioned at the start of this Chapter, I have been following this ritual **daily** now for fifteen years plus, and it is extraordinary how every morning the simple act of reciting such prayers with conviction and belief, writing in a Gratitude Journal, etc. automatically enables one's Higher Self (*Spiritual Self*) to lift them up beyond the world that they experience each day from their bodily senses. There is 'power' in participation. **Participation, full participation, is the single most powerful tool that one has for change.**

In the process of participation, being focused and reciting these words <u>**daily**</u> with passion & belief, you will slowly but surely change situations in ways you could never have imagined. But of more significance, you will subtly and slowly effect permanent change **'Within'** your Self, in how you think, speak and act. Participation, full participation, is not about control but rather the seeking of clarification and change. And then all that is required is to 'let go' of the outcome and to be disciplined and patient. Just commit and focus on this **daily habit** (i.e. the process), trust, and have faith that it is truth!

Dear God, THANK YOU for this new day, its beauty and its light. Thank You for my chance to begin again. THANK YOU, THANK YOU, THANK YOU

What a magnificent way to start your day every day! Here at the very start of your day, YOU are expressing *Thanks* for a new day. Powerful words indeed! Giving thanks that you have awakened to another day. Expressing *gratitude* for having been given the 'gift' of another day of living. There are those in this world who will not have awakened to a new day and sadly never will, for during your night's sleep there will be those somewhere in the world who have passed away for all sorts of reasons.

There will be those who will have passed away during a failed medical procedure, for example. Others will have died in road accidents or been killed from a bomb exploding in a conflict zone somewhere in the world (refer again to the picture at the front of this book). But you, my friend, have been given the privilege, the gift, to wake up and to be blessed with another new day of living. **STOP, PAUSE, REFLECT** here for a few moments and slowly re-read this headline again in order to have a deep appreciation for the 'gift' of life itself — another chance to begin the day!

How powerful is that! Is it not worth the time to **STOP,** even briefly, to **PAUSE and REFLECT** every morning, to give Thanks for such an amazing 'gift'! A gift that we all too often simply take for granted: the chance to begin again! That chance, that precious gift, which is not available to everyone! A brand-new day to start your life with a clean slate. When you **PAUSE** as you recite and think deeply on what these words are conveying to you right at this moment, make no mistake, this is extremely powerful energy at work here. Do not just take this new day for granted. It is a 'special gift' that you have been given. The 'gift' of life itself which is a very precious gift indeed, is it not? You are starting your new day on a blank page in the book or movie titled *'Your Life'* and you are free to choose how the script for that day will proceed for you.

Free Me from the Limitations of Yesterday. Today may I be Reborn

You are now asking to be freed of any limitations, weaknesses or worries that you may have had yesterday. Whatever happened in your life yesterday, good or bad, you are asking to be released from it, as you are starting a new day with a clean slate. Yesterday is gone. It is in your past. You cannot change in any way the events of yesterday. You are reborn today, a new person. Whoever you were yesterday is gone as you are now starting over brand-new today. This is the 'power of the mind' at work. You will become aware of how powerful words are when you **STOP, PAUSE, REFLECT** and think deeply on the meaning of the words as you express them!

May I become more fully a Reflection of Your Radiance

Dear God, give Me Strength, Compassion, Courage and Wisdom

You are asking now if you can reflect onto others today the goodness and grace of God/Spirit/Source/? You are asking God/Spirit/Source/? for inner **Strength** so that you can show **Compassion** to all, and for you to have **Courage & Wisdom**. These are very powerful qualities to experience in your daily life as you go about your days, weeks, months and the years ahead. Remember that most important and relevant quote: Ask and You Shall Receive. You must first Ask (as you are doing here) and then simply Let Go and continue with your day whilst being patient and gentle with your Self.

Show me the Love in My Self and in Others.

You begin to now believe and have faith in the love that you have for your 'Inner Self' (your Soul) and for others. When you begin to feel and experience miraculous change in your 'Inner Self', you will become **aware** of the love that others have for you and for their fellow man, as you do for them. You become **aware** that ALL people have the capacity to love firstly themselves, and ultimately to love all sentient beings. These are positive steps forward for all of us. When you *believe* and *have faith* in this process you are automatically listening to those *whispers of your heart* rather than to the Ego mind. But remember, this all takes time to manifest, so please be patient and just allow it to all unfold in accordance with God/Spirit/Source's/? Plan.

May I Recognise the Good that is Available Everywhere.

Despite all the bad that we see on TV and read daily in newspapers or on social media, there is 'good' everywhere and in everyone if we take the time to look deeply. Just because some of us have different coloured skin, speak a different language, wear different clothes, follow a different religion or ideology, etc. it doesn't mean that these same human beings do not have similar physical, mental, emotional and spiritual needs. Every human being has firstly the simple notion that we all want to be recognised and accepted as worthwhile individuals who want and need to be loved and appreciated for who we are and to then simply lead happy, healthy and contented lives.

As individuals, we all need to recognise and be accepting of this basic premise, and to trust that there is good in ALL human beings. Remember though that the Ego will try hard in a variety of ways to stop you from experiencing this powerful personal growth and change that will begin to manifest in your very important 'inner world'.

May I be, this day God, an Instrument of Love and Healing

How powerful is this phrase when said with conviction! Asking to be an *'instrument of love and healing'*. Think of yourself as just that as you travel to work, back home, drive on a highway, teach in a school, walk on a beach or on a bush track, work in a hospital or a shop, sit quietly on a park bench, or have lunch with a friend, etc. Today, regardless of whatever it is that you do, everything that you say and do will be done with nothing but Love & Healing in your heart. Regard yourself as an INSTRUMENT of Love and Healing. Powerful words indeed!

Lead Me into Gentle Pastures

You are asking God/Spirit/Source/? to direct your day so that you tread gently wherever you are, in whatever you say and in whatever you are doing. When you participate with conviction and energy in reciting this prayer every morning, as well as *believing and trusting* that what you are saying to be truth, then magic will happen in YOUR Life.

You will gradually feel subtle changes happening as you go about your normal day reflecting on the words in this and the other material that you read in this book. The changes in YOUR Life may not be instantaneous, but in time, as your Belief and Trust in what you are reciting develops, a subtle 'shift' will happen and the magic will flow.

Trust is something that must be earned, and only by participating fully and reciting this **daily,** will that trust slowly grow. Sometimes in life, we must have 'blind trust' or 'blind faith' in what others are teaching us. I have participated that way, and this, my friend, is one of those moments for You.

Give Me Deep Peace God So that I Might Serve You Most Deeply.

You now ask God/Spirit/Source/? to give you deep peace in your busy day, so that you may 'serve'. The key words to concentrate on here are *'peace'* and *'serve'*. You want to have a peaceful day and to serve in whatever way that you can. You must apply this powerful concept to what it is you do in YOUR day every day!

It may be to drive a bus or a train. It may be to teach in a school or university. It may be that you are a doctor, a nurse, an electrician, an IT expert or a plumber. Maybe you are an author or a retail worker or a manager. Maybe you are a kitchenhand, a cleaner or a builder. You might be a pilot, a student, a politician, a community worker, a volunteer, a hairdresser or a retired person. Whatever it is that you do **daily**, we are all meant to 'serve' in some way.

Almighty God and Guardian Angels, I Give You Thanks and Praise. Amen.

Finally, you finish the prayer as you always should, by giving Thanks and Praise. Thanks and Praise that you are alive. Thanks for all that you have. Thanks for your day ahead. As expressed throughout this book, we ALL have so much to be thankful for. But unfortunately, as I also explained earlier, many of us take so much of the good that we have in our lives for granted, and it is not until it is gone that we suddenly realise what we had to be grateful, for example, our health, our job, our home, a friend, a loved one, a special pet, a business, etc.

Just the other day, I heard the following very appropriate words as part of a song I happened to be listening to as I was driving on the motorway: 'Don't ya know it seems to be, ya just don't know what ya got 'til it's gone...' So true, but as I was driving at the time, that's all that I can remember of the song!

You must realise and accept that you cannot expect miracles overnight. You MUST just believe, commit, focus, practise, persist and be patient with these **daily** prayers. Do that and gradually over time, you will become **aware** on that Higher Spiritual level, that Higher Level of Consciousness, of the powerful and positive benefits these prayers are subtly bringing to your **daily** life. For some that realisation (*lightbulb moment*) may be almost instantaneous, and that's fantastic. But for others, let me assure you that if you participate in and trust this process **daily** and are patient with these practices, then it *WILL* ultimately happen for each of you, as it did for myself. Why wouldn't it!

When you begin to experience the power of these 'special' words in your life, you will, in due course, become aware of the subtle changes that are happening to your *'Inner Self'*. Take some time right now, my friend. Put the book down and **STOP, PAUSE, REFLECT** for ten minutes or so on what you have just learnt in this Chapter thus far. It is vitally important that you **STOP**, take some time out, be alone and **THINK** deeply on what you have just learnt. This can be a very powerful moment in YOUR life right now! It is in your hands, my friend, and whatever you choose to do is *YOUR CHOICE*, and your choice alone!

I Know That in Each
Moment I am Free
to Decide.

If My Thoughts Are
Apprehensive or
Doubtful, Then That is
What Will Show Up.
I Must Become What
I Want to Attract.

My second powerful **'Morning Prayer'** is below. Again, I will write the entire prayer and then follow up by breaking it down line by line to explain the 'power' of these words in more detail:

Dear God, I give this day to You.

May my mind stay centred on things of Spirit.

May I not be tempted to stray from love.

As I begin the day, God, I open to receive You.

Please enter where You already abide.

May my mind and heart be pure and true.

And may I not deviate from the things of goodness.

May I see the love and innocence in all mankind behind the 'masks' that we all wear and the illusions of this worldly plane.

God, I surrender to You my doings this day, I ask only that they serve You and the healing of the world.

May I bring Your love and goodness with me, to give unto others wherever I go.

Dear God, make me the person You would have me be.

Direct my footsteps and show me what You would have me do.

Make the world a safer, more beautiful place.

Bless all Your creatures.

Heal us all and use me, dear Lord, so that I may know the joy of being used by You.

Almighty God and guardian angels, I give You thanks & praise.

Amen.   (Marianne Williamson)

Dear God, I Give this Day to You

Again, what a most brilliant way to start YOUR day! You pledge to give all that you are going to do this day to God/Spirit/Source/? Obviously, you would want to give God/Spirit/Source/? only your very best, so by making this early morning pledge you are immediately attuned to starting your day with Love in your heart and with a happy, joyful attitude. Pledge to perform at your very best in whatever it is that you are going to do on this day, and then act with care and in accordance with an open, loving heart.

May My Mind Stay Centred on Things of Spirit

You are pledging that you will keep your Mind only on things of Spirit as you go about your day. And God/Spirit/Source/? would want you to be mindful/**aware** of all that you think, say, and do during your day. Mindful/**aware** of being kind, thoughtful and compassionate in all your dealings with everyone, and in everything that you may encounter during this day. If you start your day with this attitude of Love for all, then you WILL stay centred on all that is God/Spirit/Source/?

Affirm: I know that I can connect my mind with the divine mind and guarantee myself peace in any moment.

May I not be Tempted to Stray from Love

You are asking for God/Spirit/Source's help to not stray your thoughts, speech, or actions, from coming from a place other than a place of love. It is doubtless that things may arise during your day where you could easily stray in your interactions with others and act/react from a place of Fear rather than from a place of Love. You must learn to always replace Fear with Love and Trust.

When you feel yourself being tested in a situation and you can feel a sense of anger building, then giving in and 'letting go' becomes easier each time that you put the act of 'letting go' into practise. It creates an amazing sense of release to just 'let go', to be free of the anger building up. It will require practise, and you will discover how easy it becomes now that you are **aware** of how to proceed. Refer to the previous Chapter and the example of the monk in the busy airport lounge and the art of how to 'let go'.

Anger and hatred, together with the Ego, are the real enemies of <u>lasting</u> happiness.

Affirm: I know that the very essence of my being and the way of transforming my life is Love.

As I Begin the Day God, I Open to Receive You, Please Enter Where You Already Abide

As you prepare to say these words, lift and spread your arms out wide on each side of your body at the 'heart level', thereby opening your heart to receive God/Spirit/Source/? And then as you are reciting the words, bring your hands in over your heart. This action and these words spoken slowly and passionately, reinforce your belief that God/Spirit/ Source/? lives in the 'heart' of each one of us. There are no exceptions! There are only those who have not yet learned this to be true. That is until now, my friend. Until now! *Believe and Trust!* Fostering new Beliefs creates new Behaviours, which is what we are endeavouring to develop.

Affirm: I know that my higher self (spiritual self) is always ready to lift me up beyond the world that I experience with my senses.

May My Mind and Heart be Pure & True, and may I Not Deviate from the Things of Goodness

You are now confirming that you want your Heart & Mind to be free of any evil/bad thoughts, words or actions this day. You want only to partake in activities/actions that are good, not just for yourself, but also for the good of all others whom you may have contact with during this day.

Affirm: I am **aware** that I do not need to dominate anyone in order to be Spiritually Awake.

May I See the Love and Innocence in All Mankind, behind the 'masks' that We All Wear, and the Illusions of this Worldly Plane

Now, this is something that may take time for some to accept. But think about it. Every one of us has this invisible 'social mask' that we wear at times, even though most of us are either not **aware** of it or we simply do not accept that we do wear a 'mask'. (Refer back to Chapter 6 for a refresh on the Ego and 'Social Masks'.)

Affirm: I know that I am strengthened as I seek to make truth my personal reality!

God, I Surrender to You My doings this Day. I Ask only that they Serve You and the Healing of the World.

You are giving your assurance here to God/Spirit/Source/? that everything that you are going to do on this day you are giving up to Him. All your thoughts, words and actions on this day will be to help serve His Plan for you, and to help in some small way with the healing of our very troubled world.

Affirm: I will work this day at my purest intentions for the Highest good of all and I will radiate my sacred Self outwards for the collective good of all.

May I bring Your Love & Goodness with Me to give unto others Wherever I go.

You are pledging that you will give the love and goodness that is God/Spirit/Source/? to everyone that you encounter in your day wherever, and with whoever that might be. With everyone you encounter throughout your day, you should see God/Spirit/Source/? in them just as they will see God/Spirit/Source/? in you. It could be when you are standing in a queue waiting for a train and chatting with a stranger, or paying an account at a shop, or when running a business meeting or group discussion, or dealing with some issue during a telephone conversation, etc. You pledge that you will be pleasant at all times and that your energy will pass nothing but love and goodness to all those with whom you have dealings this day. <u>Remember,</u> it is always better for all concerned when one chooses to be kind, rather than the Ego's need to be right.

Affirm: I will work this day at my purest intentions for the highest good of all and I will radiate my sacred Self outwards for the collective good of all.

Dear God, Make Me the Person You would have Me Be.

This is your time each morning to ask God/Spirit/Source/? to help you to be the person that God/Spirit/Source/? wants you to be, which may not necessarily be the person who you have been working to be. You are now *surrendering that task* to God/Spirit/ Source/? who wants you to be no more than a caring, compassionate soul who does no harm to others in how you think, speak and act. And remember, for each of us, despite what plans that we may make for our life, God/Spirit/Source/? holds our **'Master Plan.'**

Affirm: I know that I am already whole and that I need not chase after anything in order to be complete!

Direct My Footsteps and Show Me what You would have Me Do.

You are surrendering all your actions this day to God/Spirit/Source/? and asking God/Spirit/Source/? what He wants you to do today. You are asking for clarity on what your life purpose is, which is typically to 'serve' in some capacity. Once you have surrendered that to God/Spirit/Source/? then you simply 'let go' of the outcome and just try to be the very best that you can be in all that you say and do on this day, as you do every day. For that is all that God/Spirit/Source/? will ever require of you.

Affirm: There is only one class of people who think more about money than the rich, and that is the poor. In fact, the poor can think of nothing else!

Make the World a Safer, more Beautiful Place.

You are asking God/Spirit/Source/? to make our physical World a safe place in which we can all live peacefully together, and for all of us to accept and be grateful for the amazing 'gifts' that this World has to offer each of us.

Affirm: I am grateful for the limitless abundance that I have in my life right now!

Bless all Your creatures.

You are asking God/Spirit/Source/? to bless all the beautiful animals, birds, insects, etc. that we have in this World.

Heal Us All, and use Me dear Lord, so that I might know the Joy of being used by You.

Finally, you are now asking God/Spirit/Source/? to heal YOU on your Soul level. To make YOU more like Him, to use all of us to bring others back to Him, and then to feel the joy that comes from being part of such a rewarding experience. Powerful words indeed!

Almighty God and Guardian Angels, I give You Thanks and Praise. Amen

Again, you give the extraordinary power of **THANKS** and **PRAISE** for all that God/Spirit/Source/? has given to you, as detailed throughout the book.

STOP, PAUSE, REFLECT for a few minutes right now on the power of the words in these first two Prayers.

We should always limit our Prayers (i.e. **powerful sentences!**) to requests for guidance and for an open heart and mind to enable us to receive, and for the awareness of the need to then act on the messages received!

It Matters Little What Others Say and Think of Me, It Matters Much What I Say and Think of Myself!

My third powerful **Morning Prayer** is a prayer from Saint Francis of Assisi (1182-1226) who was the founder of the Franciscan order of monks and who referred to ALL living beings as being his brothers and sisters. Again, when recited **daily** with *passion & belief*, it opens one's Soul to what is important in life. Which is 'to be of service'! This prayer was apparently first written some 800 years ago.

Lord make me an instrument of your peace.

Where there is hatred, let me sow love;

Where there is injury, pardon;

Where there is doubt, faith;

Where there is despair, hope;

Where there is darkness, light;

And where there is sadness, joy.

O Divine Master, grant that I may not so much seek to be consoled as to console;

To be understood as to understand;

To be loved as to love;

For it is in giving that we receive;

It is in pardoning that we are pardoned;

And it is in dying that we are born into eternal light.

(St Francis of Assisi)

Here again, a very powerful set of words that when recited **daily** over weeks and months with conviction, together with the other prayers and affirmations as set out in this book, will have an amazing, positive effect on Your life. Trust this. Believe it!

The last six or seven lines of this prayer are incredibly powerful indeed.

Please **STOP, PAUSE, REFLECT** for a few minutes right now on the powerful words in this very 'special prayer' before you continue your reading.

MAKE NO JUDGEMENTS!

HAVE NO EXPECTATIONS!

Daily, also recite the following Creed with the same *passion, conviction and belief.*

MY LIFE'S CREED

May I become at ALL times, both Now and Forever God:

A Protector for those Without Protection

A Guide for those who have Lost their Way

A Ship for those with Oceans to Cross

A Bridge for those with Rivers to Cross

A Sanctuary for those in Danger

A Lamp for those without a Light

A Place of Refuge for those who Lack Shelter

And a Servant to All in Need.

STOP, PAUSE, REFLECT now on each of these undertakings. This Creed highlights the fact that each of us can be a vessel of 'service' in helping others less fortunate than ourselves and in ALL circumstances.

This is *HOW* each of us can 'be of service' in our **daily** lives!

My Daily Practice

The following are the **EIGHT RULES** that I try to live my life in accordance with. I softly recite these Rules to myself first thing every morning with passion and conviction—a <u>**daily habit.**</u>

As you slowly and softly recite them every morning, you too will feel and become **aware** of the power that these words bring to your inner being!

<u>I CHOOSE TO LIVE MY LIFE ACCORDING TO THE FOLLOWING RULES:</u>

1. I Will Make NO Judgements
2. I Have NO Expectations
3. I Give Up The Need To Know Why Things Happen As They Do

   (This is WISDOM to Accept Things as they Are.)
4. I Trust that the Unscheduled events of our lives are a form of Spiritual direction.
5. I have the Courage to make the Choices I need to make, Accept what I cannot Change, and have the wisdom to know the difference.
6. I Choose to live my life in the Present Moment and appreciate each day for what it is—a precious gift.
7. I eat no junk food.
8. I think no junk thoughts.

Rules 1 and 2 are the Rules that I am personally tested with virtually every day and often on countless occasions throughout any day. However, the positive here is that at least I am now **aware** (remember: **The greatest weakness in life is lack of awareness**) that I may be breaching one of these Rules and I can then immediately pause and reflect on my thinking or actions, fine-tune them, and quickly adjust any undesirable mindset or activity. Over time, once you have adopted these Rules and recite them every morning, you will notice that when you then subsequently listen to the conversations of others, you too, will become acutely **aware** of how we can be, and often are, a very judgemental society.

Affirm: My judgements prevent me from seeing the good that lies beyond appearances!

Rule 3 is to give up the need to know why everything happens as it does. Simply *'Let Go'* and allow yourself to go with the flow of life! Too often many of us are spending too much time trying to understand why all sorts of things happen in our life, and so we inevitably become stressed about the smallest of issues. We sweat the small stuff! Therefore, we need to focus on the bigger picture of life, to be continuously grateful and to allow the wisdom of living a healthy, safe, joyful and contented life to flow through us. We never query for example why night always follows day, we just accept it as normal. And this is how we should accept much of what happens in our daily life. Accept life as it comes and goes, because it always does come, and then it goes on. Nothing remains the same forever. We all need to learn to relax a little, breath a lot, control our Ego, have fun, and to simply 'Go with the Flow' of life. In other words, just allow life to be!

Rule 4 is best explained with an example of what this Rule means. Allow me to briefly explain here an unscheduled event that happened in my life. On a spiritual level, it was certainly a defining **(awakening)** event in my life. And the event, as I have briefly expressed earlier, was the passing of my older brother Laurie to prostate cancer. Such a loss of a loved one can be an incredible spiritual experience in one's life, as in this instance it was for me. On that spiritual level, it was an incredibly rewarding experience when subsequent events were considered. This was a man who had worked hard in his professional career, raised a family, was admired and respected by his peers, and gave unselfishly to his local community over a long period of time.

As I was moving through the inevitable grieving period, a spiritual **awakening**, if you like, manifested. Powerful moments of discovery or reinforcement of beliefs were revealed to me. A deep sense of knowing or **awakening** to many of the realities of life and to what is important for one to understand, accept, and appreciate about life, changed the direction of my thinking and life practises as they had been up until this particularly sad event occurred. By being totally open to all that was happening, rather than resisting or blocking it, I began to acknowledge and accept that without any emotional effort on my part that there was a lot of 'inner work' going on here.

Even though I had read widely and thought that I had learnt much about life before this sad event had occurred, it was not until the loss of this very important person from my life in January 2015 that I began to have these profound **awakening** 'lightbulb' moments/revelations about what fundamentally matters in our precious life on a **daily basis.**

As time moved on and the initial emotional pain of this loss was subsiding, I began to experience a profound and deep acceptance, that, regardless of whatever material wealth one has accrued in this life, you take nothing with you when you depart. Your bank account balances revert to zero. Your real estate properties, motor vehicles, stock portfolios, your expensive designer clothes and footwear - everything right down to your toothbrush - stays behind when you depart this life. Ultimately, all that you have accumulated in this material world ends up in the possession of someone else. And for me, these spiritual lessons during this period, were stark and profound. Those *'lightbulb'* moments that I have been talking about began to shine ever so brightly!

Even though I had heard or read of many of these critical facts of life before this sad event occurred, it was not until the final departure of this loved one from my life that I was faced with having to be brutally honest and accepting of these life lessons, which has ultimately been an amazing **awakening** experience on my life journey. These facts of life include: the importance of living life in the present moment. Live for today as tomorrow is promised to no one. Also, not working too hard. (Regret number two in the book *Top Five Regrets of the Dying*, mentioned earlier.) Another fact of life is the acceptance of being able to 'Let Go', to be Grateful **daily**, and to give Thanks for life's many truly precious 'gifts'. Also, one must Surrender to what is and be grateful for ALL that you have had in your past, both the good and bad, ALL that you have now, and ALL that you may have in the future.

This event was that *unscheduled event that is a form of spiritual direction* moment in my life. And that is why this book has been written, to primarily help people to overcome that *greatest weakness in life*, as previously expressed numerous times, being: *lack of awareness!* And for many of us, it is not until such events happen in our lives that we become **aware**, or we basically *wake up!*

Rule 5 explains that by living in Western society, we have the *freedom* to make choices about how we live our lives and sometimes it requires real *courage* to make certain choices in our lives. For example, it takes courage to *choose* to spend one's life savings and invest in an established business, or in a start-up business. And then alternatively we must *accept*, for example, that we cannot change the weather or when the ocean's tides will rise or fall, etc. We need to be **aware**, and to develop the *wisdom* to know the difference here. In choosing to invest in a business one has a free choice, but in relation to the weather or the rise or fall of the tides, we must accept that we have no control over mother nature. It is wisdom to know the difference! The examples I have given here may seem to be rather simplistic, but there are no doubt other specific instances that you can think of and relate to personally.

Rule 6 is what we all must strive to make a **daily habit**, i.e. living in the present moment, for that is all that any of us has, *the present*. The past is gone and cannot be changed in any way, whilst the future is just that, a maybe, a possibility, an unknown! No one can control or be 100% sure about the future, and that is why the present is such a very precious 'gift'! Accepting this, moment by moment, is what we must all strive to achieve in our thinking, and this requires that we be completely open and honest, first and foremost with our self, and then with all in our world. To be open and honest requires courage and to be free of any guilt or blame. You must learn/practise the need to stay present and be grateful **daily** for all that you have right now (the present), rather than incessantly striving for something that you may want, but don't necessarily 'need,' at some future point in time, or what someone else has that you don't have, but want!

Living in the present is also to allow the world/ universe to be as it is, rather than as you think it should be. This grants you the comfort of *'inner peace'* by being less concerned with winning at all costs, achieving and accumulating more and more at all costs, and worrying about outcomes that you cannot control. Just remember to be present in the current moment and enjoy all the activities and pleasures that are in your life, right now.

The simple pleasure of reading and absorbing the contents of this life-changing book is a good example of being in *the present moment*. Turn off the mental 'noise' of the outside world and allow yourself the joy of just reading, and then observing your present moment thoughts right now! Do not make quick judgements (remember Rule No1) about the contents of this book for example, but rather allow the messages to resonate with your Inner Being, your *Spiritual Self*.

Rules 7 and 8 is what you have no doubt been made **aware** of at some point in your life. Eating junk food is a physical health hazard, and now be **aware**, my friend, that 'thinking junk thoughts' is a mental health hazard! Just as we need good food to fuel and nourish our bodies, so too we need healthy thoughts to fuel/nourish our minds. We source the best foods to fuel the body from organic suppliers, health shops, farmers markets, etc. and so too we should also be careful about where and from whom we source the materials vital to nourish our thoughts/our minds e.g. good bookshops, libraries, etc. And remember that brilliant quote which I included at the end of the Introduction Section of this book, which was: **'Good books are as essential to life as air is breathing!'**

STOP, PAUSE, REFLECT for a few minutes on these eight important Rules for Life!

A Healthy Body and a Healthy Mind Are Essential to Living a Fulfilling Life!

My Daily Practice

Every morning I also recite the following **'Abundance Affirmation'** which I came upon during years of seeking truth, and from which I subsequently discovered the many benefits of softly reciting it as a **daily habit**, with *passion and conviction*. It is indeed a very powerful set of words if you focus intensely on the words as you slowly whisper them to yourself. Do not just go through the motions of reciting these powerful words, but rather, concentrate and recite them with passion and conviction in your voice to manifest the magical benefits that this affirmation will ultimately bring to your life, as it has bought to mine!

ABUNDANCE AFFIRMATION

I now consciously and subconsciously flood every atom of my body, mind and spirit with Prosperity Conscious

I bless everyone in the Universe to have Abundance and Prosperity.

I give myself permission to expect Abundance and Prosperity.

I call Abundance and Prosperity from the four corners of the Earth and throughout the Universe.

Prosperity in the north, south, east and west - come to me Now!

Abundance in the north, south, east and west – come to me Now!

Money in the north, south, east, and west - come to me Now!

Riches in the north, south, east and west - come to me Now!

Wealth in the north, south, east and west - come to me Now!

Wisdom in the north, south, east and west - come to me Now!

Perfect health in the north, south, east and west - flood my entire body Now!

And So It Is, And I LOVE IT! - And I give THANKS, THANKS, THANKS.

From the God/Goddess of my being I give Thanks for the Love that I am. I give Thanks for the Love in my life and for the Love that surrounds Me. Thank You, Thank You, Thank You

Thank You for the Miracle of life that I am and for the Miracle of life that I see all around Me. Thank You for the precious 'gift' of life. Thank You, Thank You, Thank You.

Thank You for my perfect body, my health and vitality.

Thank You, Thank You, Thank You.

My Daily Practice

Thank You for the Abundance that I am and for the abundance that I see all about me. Thank You for the riches and the richness of my life and Thank You for the river of money that flows to me. Thank You, Thank You, Thank You.

Thank You for the excitement and the adventure of the millions of wondrous possibilities and probabilities. Thank You, Thank You, Thank You.

Thank You for the beauty and the harmony. Thank You for the peace and tranquillity. Thank You for the wonderment and Thank You for the Joy. Thank You for the laughter and the play. And Thank You for the privilege of serving and sharing the 'gift' that I am. Thank You, Thank You, Thank You.

(Prosperity Coaches)

This is an Affirmation which MUST be recited <u>**daily**</u> as part of the transformational journey that you will now be on.

Commit to it as a <u>**daily habit.**</u>

<u>Remember:</u> **Habits** develop **Beliefs**. **Beliefs** develop **Behaviour**.

Recite this Affirmation in a loud whisper if possible, for that is when you will not only hear, but feel, the conviction in your voice and within your Inner Self!

STOP, PAUSE, REFLECT.

Take some time again right at this point, as it is very important that you think deeply on the words of this *incredibly powerful* affirmation.

Then, of course, at the end of each day, we are to give **THANKS** for our day. My 'night prayer', as set out below, is recited AFTER I am in bed and have turned off the light, however, you can say it wherever and whenever it suits you. Lying on my back in bed with my eyes lightly closed, I always inhale and exhale two or three deep breaths to 'let go' of ALL outer world thinking/noise, and to relax and focus fully on what I am about to recite. This is important because I want my statement of Thanks to God/Spirit/Source/? to be intense and to be originating from the heart. I then, very slowly and with deep concentration, recite the following Prayer.

Dear God,

Thank you for the day.

Thank you for my safety and for the safety of my loved ones.

As I enter sleep, dear God, may these hours give me peace.

May they bring healing to my mind and to my body.

My Daily Practice

Dear God, please bless the world.

Where there is pain, where there are people who have no place to sleep, people who suffer and who die, may your angels come unto them and minister to their hearts.

Dear God, please let the light (love) stream in.

Please use my hours of rest and prepare me during these hours of rest for greater service to You.

May the love/light that surrounds me tomorrow shine through me.

Soften my heart, dear God.

I praise you and give you thanks.

Amen. (Marianne Williamson)

As with the first two 'Morning Prayers', I will now breakdown this prayer and elaborate on the 'power' of the words in it. It is the power of these words that will manifest change in YOUR life when they are recited with passion, and a resolute **BELIEF** in what you are saying to be the Truth!

Dear God/Spirit/Source, Thank You for the Day

You are speaking directly with God/Spirit/Source/? and expressing those two extremely powerful words: *THANK YOU*. You have made it through to the end of another day and, for that alone, one needs to be grateful — EVERY day! There are many in the world who will not make it home this night to be with their family. Just **STOP** for a moment and think about that!

Thank You for My Safety and for the Safety of My Loved Ones

You are Thanking God/Spirit/Source/? for your safety in all your activities throughout the day whatever they may have been. For example, if you have been away from your home today at some point and you have come back safely, then surely one should give Thanks for that. Safe travel is not something to just be taken for granted, as many of us have no doubt done in the past, that is until now when we have suddenly been made **aware** of this fact. Also, in this moment as you say these words, quickly think of the names and/or faces of 'special' people in your life and give Thanks for them also being home safe this day.

As I enter sleep dear God/Spirit/Source/? may these Hours give Me Peace.

Asking (remember you must: Ask before you Receive) that it is part of God/Spirit/Source's Plan for you that you now have a peaceful and restful night's sleep. If you are not regularly sleeping peacefully, then you must Ask that it be a part of God's Plan for you. Do not just think that it will always happen automatically. Whatever concerns or worries that you may still have as you prepare for sleep, 'Let them Go and Let God'. Ask for God/Spirit/Source/? to deal with them in accordance with **His Plan** whilst you sleep peacefully. This **daily** practice works for me, so why wouldn't it work for YOU!

May they bring Healing to My Mind and to My Body

You are now Asking that it be a part of God's Plan for you that your Body, Mind and Spirit rest peacefully and heal during your hours of sleep.

Dear God, please Bless the World

Asking God/Spirit/Source/? to bless and heal our World and to reduce the suffering for many who are currently suffering in some way. You may wish to pause for a moment and visualise someone whom you know personally to be suffering at this time. We are not just focusing on our Self in this prayer. We are also showing care, compassion and kindness for all in the world, including the animals, the oceans, the forests, and all of nature.

You are Asking God/Spirit/Source/? to send Earth Angels (people like you and I) to the Sick, the Homeless, and to all those who are Suffering. Earth angels offer care, love and support, and they pray for those who have died so that they may rest in peace in God/Spirit/Source's care.

Dear God/Spirit/Source/? please let the Light (love) shine in. Please use My hours of Rest, and prepare Me during these hours of Rest for greater service to You

Asking God/Spirit/Source/? to let the love (light) from all around you shine into your body, mind and soul whilst you sleep. Furthermore, you are asking that during these hours of restful, peaceful sleep, that God/Spirit/Source/? prepares you to be of greater service to Him when you wake again and go about your next day.

May the Love that surrounds Me, Tomorrow Shine through Me

You are Asking God/Spirit/Source/? that all the love and light that surrounds you, may it shine through you tomorrow so that you then go about your activities again with nothing but loving kindness and compassion for all in your heart.

Soften My Heart dear God/Spirit/Source

Asking that it be a part of God's/Spirit's/Source's Plan for you that your heart will soften whilst you sleep, and that you will 'Let Go' of any anger or harsh thoughts that you may be holding onto in relation to someone or something that may have eventuated during your day. You can now have that restful, peaceful sleep that your body, mind and soul desperately require each day.

I Praise You and give You Thanks. Amen

Closing your prayer again with those two powerful words: **Thank You.** Giving Praise and Thanks to God/Spirit/Source/? for your day is a superb way to sign off before restful, peaceful sleep sets in.

You may find that if you are extremely tired you might drift off to sleep before you have finished this prayer. That is okay. Do not struggle with this outcome. Do not beat yourself up. What is important though is that you make the effort **daily** to be GRATEFUL for another day of living and to give THANKS. God/Spirit/Source/? is fine with you drifting off to sleep in the middle of the prayer. It is your intention, your commitment to make the effort **daily**, and to realise the importance of finishing your day with a prayer of THANKS and PRAISE that's important. Rest easy!

This entire Chapter is the process/procedure that I go through EVERY day. And it is this daily repetition that has *created the Habits*, which *developed the Beliefs*, which *changed my Behaviour* and moulded me into the person I am today! Should you choose to adopt this same procedure, and I sincerely hope that you do, then you too will experience positive life-changing behaviour patterns developing for yourself.

LISTEN TO YOUR INNER VOICE OF WISDOM

Chapter 8
Affirmations and Teachings of Buddha

"I will work this day at my purest intentions for the highest good of all and I will radiate my sacred Self outwards for the collective good of all.'
– (Author Unknown)

For your benefit, I am now listing a small collection from the many powerful affirmations that I have collected over my many years of studying inspirational material from various 'spiritual warriors' as referenced in the Acknowledgement Section of the book. I encourage YOU to develop the **daily habit** of reciting each of these, or similar affirmations.

STOP, PAUSE, REFLECT for a few moments at the end of each affirmation to allow your mind to absorb the *'power of the words'* that you have just read.

In time, you will no doubt add other affirmations that you will uncover on YOUR inspirational and spiritual journey.

It is in this 'gap' when you **STOP, PAUSE, REFLECT** and consciously allow yourself time to absorb what you have just read, before reading the next affirmation that you will be elevated to that higher level of consciousness and at that point you will experience that important **awareness** that we are ALL seeking.

I read the affirmation once, then I close my eyes and slowly whisper it again. It is this *repetition* that, over time, enables the words to go *deep within*, to touch the Soul!

The Affirmations

I know that in each moment, <u>I am free to decide</u>.

It is impossible to be negative if I am <u>always Grateful</u>.

Awareness is all that I am seeking. and <u>awareness comes from Within</u>.

Our gift in Life is <u>the inner power</u> that we ALL have to become <u>Aware</u>.

I know that no matter how much I protest, <u>I am totally responsible</u> for everything that happens to me in my life.

My past is nothing more than <u>the trail that I have left behind</u>. What drives my life today is the '<u>energy</u>' that I generate in each of my <u>present moments</u>.

I rid myself of my doubts by remembering that there is a valid reason for <u>everything</u> that happens.

I realise that I am <u>always free to 'let go'</u> and observe my life.

I know that <u>I am already whole</u> and that I need not chase after anything in order to be complete.

<u>My judgements</u> prevent me from seeing the good that lies beyond appearances.

I know that the very essence of my being and the way of <u>transforming my life is Love</u>.

<u>The more I listen</u>, the more profound the silence becomes.

I know that my <u>Higher Self (Spiritual Self) is always ready to lift me up</u> beyond the world that I experience with my senses.

I know that I can connect my mind with the <u>Divine Mind</u> and guarantee myself <u>Peace in any moment</u>.

I know that <u>I am strengthened</u> as I seek to make <u>Truth</u> my personal reality.

I am aware that I <u>do not need to dominate anyone</u> in order to be Spiritually awake.

I will work this day at my purest intentions, for <u>the highest good of all</u>, and I will radiate <u>my Sacred Self outwards</u> for the <u>collective good of all</u>.

<u>Wisdom</u> comes to you when you are Still.

It is imperative that you are open to receiving the powerful message that **EACH** affirmation is offering, and that you are constantly aware that your Ego may well fight to block you from nurturing your Soul and achieving the spiritual growth that will follow this **<u>daily habit</u>**. Make the commitment, persist **<u>daily</u>**, be patient, and positive change will happen! It is that routine of doing it all **<u>daily</u>** that will create the Habits, which then creates the Belief, which ultimately leads to positive changes in your Behaviour!

MY EXTERNAL WORLD IS A REFLECTION OF MY INNER WORLD

Teachings of Buddha

'Those who Know do not Speak.
Those who Speak do not Know.'
(Lao-Tzu)

The Fourteen Teachings of Buddha

1. **The greatest Enemy in life is the Self.**
2. The greatest Ignorance in life is Deceit.
3. The greatest Failure in life is Vanity.
4. The greatest Tragedy in life is Jealousy.
5. The greatest Error in life is to lose Oneself.
6. The greatest Crime in life is disloyalty to Parents.
7. The greatest Pity in life is Self-belittlement.
8. The greatest Pride in life is recovering from Failures.
9. The greatest Bankruptcy in life is Hopelessness.
10. **The greatest Wealth in life is Health and Wisdom.**
11. The greatest Debt in life is Affection and Love.
12. **The greatest Gift in life is Acceptance and Forgiveness.**
13. **The greatest Weakness in life is lack of Awareness.**

14. The greatest Consolation in life is Charity.

From these fourteen Teachings of Buddha, I have chosen four that I personally have found to be extremely powerful.

<mark>STOP, PAUSE, REFLECT</mark> and think intensely on how relevant and vitally important these Teachings are. They are ALL important, of course, but the four below I personally find extremely powerful.

1. The greatest Enemy in life is the Self.
2. The greatest Wealth in life is Health and Wisdom.
3. The greatest Gift in life is Acceptance and Forgiveness.
4. The greatest Weakness in life is the lack of Awareness.

Let me elaborate on each of these four in more detail.

The Greatest Enemy in Life is the Self.

This teaching I have discussed in some detail at various stages throughout the book, but I want to reinforce again here the vital importance of being **aware** of this universal fact, and why it is necessary that one fully understands and accepts this universal truth! I have observed that many tend to struggle to accept and understand that one can be their own worst enemy. It requires first and foremost that one MUST be completely open and honest with one's Self for it is about the Ego. And for that reason, many do struggle with that. As explained earlier, every one of us has an Ego. And as explained back in Chapter 6 the Ego is that little 'voice' in our head which constantly works away every minute of our non-sleeping time.

'Your authentic Self's evil twin is the Ego"' – (Sarah ban Breathnach)

The single biggest challenge that we will all have in life, and that we may have been **unaware** of until reading this book, is learning how to dissolve, or to at least how to control, our Ego. It will be working right now as you read this, and for some, your Ego may well be saying, "I don't believe what I am reading here. I know what's best for me." If that is happening for you right now, then that is your Ego at work! And this is one of the biggest challenges that any of us will ever have, learning HOW to 'control' that Ego. The Ego's first reaction is for you to focus on the messenger (in this instance, the author of this book) and to forget about the message! However, I implore you to accept that it is vital that you focus on this important message and not on the messenger! After all, Buddha was an exceptionally wise man!

The Greatest Wealth in life is Health and Wisdom.

In relation to our health, if we do not have excellent health, both physically and mentally, then we are certainly not wealthy. We may have a wealth of material assets, but the two greatest assets that any of us can possibly have, are brilliant physical and mental health. If/when we lose our mental and/or physical health then, regardless of our material wealth, we may not necessarily be able to regain that optimum health back.

Therefore, it is critical that we become aware (there is that **'awareness'** factor again) of how well we look after the body that God/Spirit/Source/? blessed us with, and that we do all that we can to ensure that we maintain optimum levels of physical and mental health at all times. One only need think of the people that they hear or read about who are millionaires, even billionaires, who have deep struggles with their mental and/or physical health and wellbeing. Reflect for a moment or two right now on your own position in relation to this critical matter. Again, please be completely open and honest with yourself, as it is YOUR physical and mental wellbeing that matters!

'The first wealth is health.' – (Ralph Waldo Emerson)

Be aware that if you have nothing in your life other than excellent health, you are wealthy. To confirm this claim just ask any patient in a cancer ward in any hospital or in a hospice.

Wisdom, of course, is striving to reach that higher level of consciousness, of simply being **aware**. Wisdom is knowledge and truth manifested as clarity of vision. Wisdom is knowing that there is more to a wholesome, joyful and fulfilled life than just accumulating the rewards of material successes. Dr Wayne Dyer once said, "There is a difference between knowing about God, and knowing God." When you arrive at that point in your life when you understand and accept this statement, and you know that you know God (i.e. you know you have a 'connection' with God), then you will be **aware** that you have reached a higher level of consciousness, and you will feel that from **Within**.

Wisdom is being **aware**/knowing/believing and accepting, that <u>**lasting happiness, inner peace and contentment**</u> can only come from **'Within!** Wisdom is not needing to know why things happen as they do, but rather, accepting things as they are. When you do that, you can be content, happy and maintain 'inner peace'. To maintain optimum Health and Wisdom it is critical that you regularly **STOP, PAUSE, REFLECT** on how you Think, Speak and Act (i.e. you **Look Within**).

The Greatest GIFT in life is Acceptance and Forgiveness.

It is our greatest gift to accept things as they are without always searching for a reason as to why it is so. As a small example, you might be retrenched from a job that you love. First, you must **accept** that it has happened, grieve if you must, but accept it as reality because it is! Let it go, put it behind you and move on with your life, because you must. Accept that bad 'stuff' happens to everyone—that is part of life. When you have learnt to accept that the past is nothing more than the trail that you have left behind, what will always drive your life from this moment forward is the energy that you will generate in each of your present moments! Simply 'Let Go', have courage, have faith, believe in yourself, and move forward. Regardless of what you may wish to happen, you cannot go back. The past is just that, past. The sun will rise again, day will follow night, the tides will rise and fall, the waves will continue to roll in, and you will find a better job, etc. It's all part of **God's Master Plan** for YOU!

Whatever troublesome issues that you may have in your days, weeks, months and years ahead, you must learn to accept them as part of life. And for those that you have had in your past let them go! They are nothing more than the lesson's that God/Spirit/Source/? is sending for you to learn from. And remember, *everything in life happens for a reason.* You may not immediately understand the reason/lesson, but, in time, you will. Forgive anyone or anything that causes you discomfort, 'Let Go' and move on. When you truly forgive from the heart, good will come to you. Learning to forgive and to 'let go' is an incredibly important part of living a happy, contented, peaceful and fulfilled life.

If you are angry with someone, an easy way of letting go of that anger is to think of anger being like you drinking poison and then hoping that the other person gets sick or dies! Your anger affects only you, not them. Another way of looking at anger is if someone has said something that upsets you, remember this slogan that I learnt back in my secondary school days: **'Sticks and stones can break my bones, but words cannot hurt me, unless I let them.'** Choose not to allow someone's harsh words to have a negative effect on how you think and act. Another person's words cannot affect you unless, YOU let them!

The Greatest Weakness in life is Lack of AWARENESS.

This is the big one, of course, and possibly the most important. Our greatest weakness, as previously expressed numerous times, is our lack of **awareness!** And the most crucial issue that we need to confront and be 100% honest with, is that initially many of us are not even **aware** that we are not **aware!** Hence, for many, this can be a difficult proposition to confront and, more importantly, to accept. This approach may be the unfortunate result of having stopped reading good books! <u>Remember:</u> **reading good books is as important as breathing is to life.**

The Ego will fight hard to deny that one is not **aware** because, as also previously explained, the Ego does NOT like change, and **awareness** results in change—a change in your thinking! Remember the sub-heading of this book: *Change Your Thinking, Change Your Life.* The Ego doesn't like personal development, growth and nurturing of the Soul, and that is why your Ego may not be agreeable to you reading this book.

Always remember that *change is inevitable, but personal growth is an option.* Personal growth and spiritual development are a free choice that one always has available to them! Acceptance in your life of not being fully **aware** can evolve into a significant turning point in your life, should you be totally honest with yourself and accept it to be true. For me, as it maybe for you, I was not **aware** that I was not **aware**, until I made a commitment to myself to become a 'spiritual seeker' which, once commenced, slowly evolved into being a 'spiritual warrior', and ultimately became my life's passion. One simply becomes a 'seeker of truth'.

Affirm: Wisdom comes when you are Still and sitting in Silence.

BE PATIENT AND OPEN TO THE IDEAS OF OTHERS

Chapter 9:
Masters Achievers

'Learn to Let Go. That is the key to happiness.'
– (Buddha)

Master Achievers are
- \# Accountable
- \# Responsible
- \# Ownership

The Victims
- \# Deny
- \# Defend
- \# Justify
- \# Blame

(eQ events)

What does all this mean? What is the significance of the above table?

Well, it is simply about being **aware** of all that you say and do in YOUR **daily** life, minute by minute. You must continuously ask yourself if what you say, or how you act, are ABOVE the line (**Master Achievers**) or BELOW the line (**Victims**). That is all this is. Simply being **aware** of where you stand in this regard when you speak or act. You should always strive to be a *Master Achiever*. In other words, to be Accountable, to be Responsible and to take Ownership of all that you say and do. However, too many of us often tend to take 'the Victim' option. Why? Because it is often the easier option!

When something happens in our day and we are brought to account for what we have said or how we have acted in a certain situation, then it can be the easier option for us to just play the *Victim*. We deny that we said it or did it, defend what we said or did, justify what we said or did, or blame someone else or some other circumstance for what we said or did.

It is important that we all accept that there will have been occasions in our past where we have taken *the Victim* option because it saved us from embarrassment, or this option saved us from having to honestly deal with the outcome of what we had said or done. This is normal. It happens to all of us. After all, no one lives above the line

24/7 for 365 days of the year, year after year! And that is okay. Even *Master Achievers* have lapses. No one is perfect. Perfection in anything does not exist, so don't beat yourself up. The advantage is, however, now that you are **aware** (remember that importance of being **aware**) of how this practice works, it should always be your goal to operate by living your life ABOVE the line **daily!**

Choosing to live your life in this manner is what makes you a more worthwhile and valuable human being. We are all, or can be, *Master Achievers*. We are Accountable, Responsible, and take Ownership of our actions and what we say. Subsequently, we are proud of who we are, regardless of what anyone else may think or say about us! We are learning to live an authentic life, just as we are meant to do. Exciting isn't it!

Sadly though, many will still choose to travel through much, if not their entire life, living BELOW the line. They will choose the easier path of denying or defending or justifying or blaming someone else or some other circumstance for what they said or did, or for where they are in their life. Rather than choosing the possibly more difficult but honest and appropriate option of being accountable and responsible for what they said or did, and to take ownership of it. One cannot expect to live a life of lasting happiness, inner peace and contentment if they continually fail to be responsible and accountable for what they say and do. Sorry, but life just does not work like that!

Now that you have learnt this practical process and are **aware** of the practise required for authentic living, always choose to live your life *ABOVE* the line. You will automatically love yourself and others even more when you do! Again, it is *vital* that you be completely open and honest with yourself when reflecting on this proposition. Make it a **daily habit**, to live your life in the present moment - *ABOVE the line!*

To assist you in always striving to be a Master Achiever you could start by adopting the **eight Rules** for daily living as set out in Chapter 8. This may well be a good starting point for you. However, in time, you may desire to refine these Rules as you slowly and confidently develop your own Rules. I certainly encourage you to develop and adopt your own Rules for authentic living. The point is, you should develop your own Rules and Beliefs for YOUR life, and not just comply with those suggested for you by myself or by others. However, the idea here is that you initially consider the benefits of adopting into your **daily** living the proven ideas and concepts of others, as described in this book for example, until you are confident about developing your own Rules.

The Rules that *YOU* want to live *YOUR* life in accordance with ultimately should fit with who YOU are, who YOU choose to be and not who others think you should be! That is the crux of this entire book. For the reader to **Look Within** and to freely decide what beliefs, faith and values they want to live their very precious life in accordance with. You have that option to freely choose. If you fail to act and to make changes, then that action too is a choice that you will have freely made. Remember that quote of Zig Ziglar that I gave in the Introduction section of the book:

'If you always do as you have always done, then you will always get what you have always got.'

I have added further suggestions that you may choose to include as you build your very own set of Rules and strive to be a Master Achiever.

1. <u>**Remember to rest and calm your mind every morning and/or every evening.**</u>

Do this **daily** and you will experience changes in your life that currently you may not think possible. You will learn that being still and calming the mind is the only time that messages can reach you on your Soul level. Ralph Waldo Emerson once wrote, **'There are voices which we hear in solitude, but they grow faint as we enter the world.'** It is *vital* that, at some point in your day, every day, you find the time to sit in silence, to shut-out all the 'noise' of the outside material world, and just sit, in silence.

That means no television, no radio, no music, no social media, no internet at all, no phone calls, no reading, etc. Just sit in silence for 10-15 minutes as a minimum, and quiet your mind! For it is only when you sit in this space of silence that your 'inner voice', your Soul, will hear the messages that God/Spirit/Source/? is constantly sending to you. If one does not find this 'space' **daily**, this silent short 'gap' in their day, then the messages will continue to be received, but will be done so via mistakes, stumbles, blunders, errors, misadventures, etc.

If you have studied this book as it has been written, and you have refrained from being rigid in your assessment or judgement of what you have read (i.e. your Ego is NOT in control), then you should understand by now the benefits of choosing to make this practise a part of your **daily** life—an integral part of who you are!

Furthermore, as I have stressed throughout the book, things will not change overnight as this is not some magical quick fix solution to all your issues in life. Positive change does not necessarily come quickly. It requires ongoing effort (reward follows effort). With constant, determined application, we can all accomplish the most difficult of goals. Be patient, be gentle, and do not expect too much too soon.

Remember **Rule 2** of those eight Rules for life: *Have no expectations!* Just like an oak tree, which does not grow overnight, you need to nourish your Soul with spiritual and emotional 'food' to grow, over time. One needs to rest **daily** and take 'time out' to reflect on their heart's true feelings and desires (i.e. the *'whispers of your heart'*). As previously stated, it is only when sitting in silence, preferably amid quiet surroundings, that you will receive the vital messages that you need!

It is about practising the life skill of **Looking Within, daily,** and you can only do that when the mind is calm and at rest. 'Let Go' of all worldly thoughts and pressures that have been going on outside of yourself, and simply 'Surrender' to the present moment. Make it a **daily habit** to find time to sit quietly, in solitude, and turn your attention to YOU.

2. <u>**You were born to be Real, not to be Perfect.**</u>

Do not live your life based on what you think others may say or think of you. Remember the quote that you have read numerous times throughout this book and I will repeat it again here. Write it down on pieces of paper or sticky-notes and leave it in places where you will constantly see it until it becomes a *Rule in YOUR life*.

It matters little what others say and think of Me, it matters much what I say and think of Myself.

Try always to live your life by that Rule, because if you say and think highly of yourself, then others who matter in YOUR life will think so too. You must first love and respect yourself before you can have others love and respect you. And remember that it is okay to fail. We all have failures in our lives. We all make mistakes. That is just a part of life. Mistakes are life lessons. Life is not perfect, and it never will be. Life is just that, life. *Strive for growth in your life, not perfection.* In most Western democracies, we get to choose how we live our life. Be courageous, let the failures and mistakes go, learn from them, but keep moving forward.

In his very popular book, *Rich Dad, Poor Dad,* **Robert Kiyosaki** talks in detail about why it is so important for all of us to develop *'financial intelligence'* as a life skill. To this day, such an important life skill still receives little if any dedicated attention in our higher school systems. I believe that *'spiritual intelligence'* is an equally vital life skill, but unfortunately, it receives even less attention in these very same school systems. In fact, the mere mention of the word 'spiritual' or God, in most school systems today, immediately conjures up images and thought processes for most school leaders of it all being about religion and/or religious institutions. Spirituality is not necessarily about religion or religious beliefs, but rather, it is about much of what you have been reading in this book!

3. **<u>Live boldly and give yourself permission to be happy EVERY day.</u>**

Look at that picture at the front of the book **<u>daily</u>** and immediately REFLECT on a deep level how fortunate you are to live where you do. Put things into perspective. It is highly likely that you do not live amongst regular bombings and mass destruction. So, for that reason alone, be grateful every day. Buy a **Gratitude Journal** and write in it at least **five things** that you are grateful for, **<u>daily</u>**. Make this a **<u>daily habit</u>**, a Rule to live by. It does require time, focus, commitment and effort, because we can all get busy with our lives doing 'stuff'. It is so important to be **aware** that: *Reward always follows Effort!*

Do not carry toxic mental baggage or toxic people with you throughout your precious life. Regardless of what you say or do, day will always follow night, ocean tides will always rise and fall, life will go on! Live your life every day, living at your very best! You never know when it may be your last day on this planet, and your life is what YOU make of it. *YOU are the leader in YOUR life!* Life is no dress rehearsal and your life clock is ticking! Live in the here and now, the present, today! Make peace and be gentle with yourself, and with others. If you are doing the best that you can **daily**, be proud of YOU!

Sit in that silence at some point every day, preferably in solitude, and reflect on the multitude of 'gifts' that YOU have in YOUR life right now! Gifts like having a pulse, of being able to move and breathe freely, see, speak and hear clearly, and many other gifts like those that you have previously read in this book. When this **daily** practice of **Looking Within** becomes a part of who you are, a part of your core belief system and a part of your **daily** behaviour, you will be inspired to do great things! I am inspired thinking of you practising the procedures and habits as outlined in this book, **daily** because I know what the results will be. Be grateful for this book and for this precious moment in your life, for having read the book may just be a magical light bulb moment for you!

Remember: It is the repetition that will *Change Your Thinking,* which in due course, will *Change Your Life!*

4. Create Daily Habits like those I have outlined in the book.

This is what this entire book is about, creating **DAILY HABITS** that will ensure that in due course these will become your norm, and you will become your authentic self, living your life in accordance with *the whispers of YOUR heart*.

In summary, I am writing here the **ten daily habits** that I have adopted into my **daily** life, and for which I recommend that you too initially adopt on your journey to manifest that **lasting happiness, inner peace and contentment** that we ALL desire. Then, as you progress over time, you may choose to incorporate other habits into your **daily** life, which is what I encourage you to do.

All of this will work best for you if you DO NOT try to incorporate all ten habits into your **daily** routine at the one time. I suggest, for example, that you start with **Habit 1** and practise that **daily** for 14-21 days then adopt **Habit 2**. Now you would practice both Habits 1 and 2 for the next 14-21 days, before introducing **Habit 3**, and so on. The reason that you should adopt this approach is that it takes time and patience to adopt all ten habits into your changed **daily** routine. Simply persist with this practice **daily**, be patient, and allow change to subtly evolve.

Habit 1   **BEING GRATEFUL...**

Habit 2   **LOOKING WITHIN...**

Habit 3   **LETTING GO OF THE PAST...**

Habit 4   **PERSONAL RESPONSIBILITY...**

Habit 5   **THE PRESENT MOMENT...**

Habit 6   **THE POWER OF WORDS...**

Habit 7   **8 RULES FOR LIFE...**

Habit 8   **ABUNDANCE & AFFIRMATIONS...**

Habit 9   **LIVING ABOVE THE LINE...**

Habit 10 **TAKING 'TIME OUT'...**

And as you are now **aware,** all ten of these habits have been discussed in much detail throughout the book. This is where the practice of using 'sticky notes' and a felt-tip pen, will help you to refer back to the relevant page(s) for commentary on each of these **<u>daily</u>** habits.

YOUR MIND CAN TRANSCEND ALL LIMITATIONS. YOU WILL THEN ENTER A WORLD WHERE ANYTHING IS POSSIBLE!

Chapter 10: Inviting Abundance into Your Life and Avoiding Health Imbalances

'I know that my Higher Self (Spiritual Self) is always ready to lift me up beyond the world that I experience with my Senses.'
– (Dr Wayne Dyer)

ABUNDANCE AFFIRMATION

I now Consciously and Subconsciously flood every atom of my Body, Mind & Spirit with Prosperity Consciousness.

I bless everyone in the Universe to have Abundance and Prosperity.

I give myself permission to expect Abundance and Prosperity.

I call Abundance and Prosperity from the four corners of the Earth and throughout the Universe.

Prosperity in the north, south, east and west - come to me now!

Abundance in the north, south, east and west – come to me now!

Money in the north, south, east, and west - come to me now!

Riches in the north, south, east and west - come to me now!

Wealth in the north, south, east and west - come to me now!

Wisdom in the north, south, east and west - come to me now!

Perfect health in the north, south, east and west - flood my entire body now!

And so it is and I LOVE IT!

And I give THANKS, THANKS, THANKS.

From the God/Goddess of my being, I give Thanks for the Love that I am. I give Thanks for the Love in my life and for the Love that surrounds me. Thank You, Thank You, Thank You

Thank You for the miracle of life that I am and for the miracle of life that I see all about me. Thank You for the precious 'gift' of life. Thank You for my perfect body, my health and vitality. Thank You, Thank You, Thank You.

Thank You for the Abundance that I am and for the abundance that I see all about me. Thank You for the riches and the richness of my life and Thank You for the river of money that flows to me. Thank You, Thank You, Thank You.

Thank You for the excitement and the adventure of the millions of wondrous possibilities and probabilities. Thank You, Thank You, Thank You.

Thank You for the beauty and the harmony. Thank You for the peace and tranquillity. Thank You for the wonderment and Thank You for the Joy. Thank You for the laughter and the play. And Thank You for the privilege of serving and sharing the 'gift' that I am.

Thank You! Thank You! Thank You!

This **ABUNDANCE AFFIRMATION** was included back in Chapter 7 as part of my daily prayer routine in the 'My Daily Practise' chapter. When you whisper this affirmation **daily**, with passion and conviction, you are opening your heart and mind to receiving into your life all that you *need*, and you accept that it may not necessarily be identical to that which you may *want*.

You are giving thanks for the love that is in your life and for all the love that surrounds you. When you

STOP, PAUSE, REFLECT and think deeply about this you realise (become **aware**) and appreciate the love that is all around you in the present moment. You must accept the importance of regularly stopping and thinking about this *vital message*, and how fortunate you are to receive such a message. You need to be disciplined and concentrate 100% on the words that you are reciting. It is then, and only then, that you will feel on your Soul level ('Inner Self') the *power of the words* that you are reciting.

STOP, PAUSE, REFLECT and think of the abundance that you have in your life right now. Maybe it's the abundance of energy and good health that you enjoy. The abundance of natural resources, for example, clean air to breath, clean, fresh, and running hot and cold water, electricity at the flick of a switch, regular sunshine, clean oceans to swim in, forests to walk in, gardens in which to stop and smell the flowers, and much, much more.

You must learn to take the time **daily, to STOP to PAUSE and to REFLECT,** in order to acknowledge and appreciate the abundance of these natural 'gifts' that you have available to you every day! The more that you appreciate the abundance of these gifts and recognise how important the process of constantly **Looking Within** is, then the sooner you will become **aware** of how **lasting happiness, inner**

peace and contentment can and will manifest in your life!

By acknowledging and being grateful for all the wondrous possibilities and probabilities that are available to you **daily**, you will automatically invite more of the same into your life. You are becoming **aware** that so many possibilities are readily available to you, and you must simply just practise the art of ASKING! The important thing here is to realise that to have abundance manifest in your life, in whatever shape that you want it to be revealed, you must participate fully in *the process of Asking*.

Remember:

Full participation guarantees positive results, and

Reward always follows Effort!

Make the effort and adopt these **daily habits** into YOUR life, and I can promise you that you will NOT be disappointed!

HEALTH IMBALANCES

'I know that the very essence of my being and the way of transforming my life, is LOVE.'
– (Author Unknown)

According to Tibetan medicine, human health imbalances (ill health) are due to FOUR primary mental afflictions, which they refer to as the Four Poisons:

IGNORANCE
ATTACHMENT
ANGER
RESISTANCE TO CHANGE

What this means is that because we are **IGNORANT** of the Truth, we then 'think' that we can be happy by our **ATTACHMENT** to a specific Person, Place, Thing or Feeling. Inevitably, we can be disappointed, and **ANGER**, dislike or even hatred then rears its ugly head. At that point, we have a tendency to **RESIST CHANGE** and we continue hanging onto our negative habits and frozen behaviour patterns.

REMEMBER: *If we always do as we have always done, then we will always get what we have always got.*

STOP, PAUSE, REFLECT for a few moments on what you have just read! Put the book down and think deeply on this very important truth. It can take quality time and deep reflection before one becomes fully **aware** of the power of the above statement. I have found that when I now observe people ('people watch') who regularly complain about certain negative issues that keep manifesting in their life, I notice that they often tend to continue to act the very same way regardless of the outcome, but, for some unknown reason, they expect a different result! Life just does not work like that! **'If your thoughts are apprehensive or doubtful, then that is what will show up. You must become what you want to attract!'** We are what we think. It is *vital* that you Believe and Trust this universal Truth!

When you think deeply on this message being conveyed to you here, you will become **aware** (there's that **awareness** thing again) that this is Truth, and it is why so many continually have struggles even to the point that ill health, depression, self-abuse, etc. can develop in their life. At the core of many of our problems is not the loss of someone or some object, but rather, our 'attachment' to whatever it was that is suddenly no longer in our lives. We tend to resist making changes, and we just continue doing the very same things day in and day out, but we expect a different outcome! Life does NOT work like that!

However, when we become **aware**, that if we keep holding onto our negative habits and/or frozen behaviour patterns, whatever they may be, then it is obvious that we are going to get the same results! If our thoughts and actions do not change, then why should we anticipate a different outcome/result? Again, remember that brilliant Zig Ziglar quote: **'If you always do as you have always done, then you will always get what you have always got.'**

I REALISE THAT I AM ALWAYS FREE TO 'LET GO' AND OBSERVE MY LIFE.

Again, take a few minutes and allow the power of the words that you just read to resonate before you read on!

> **'Don't look for Miracles. See everything in your life as a Miracle.'**
> **– (Chinese Proverb)**

Having read to this point, you will now be **aware** that you may have to reassess much of what you have learnt about life up until this point in time. Furthermore, you will also now be **aware**, and accept, I hope, that to achieve maximum benefit from the processes outlined in this book, it is *vital* that you are always completely open and honest with yourself when adopting into your life the **daily habits** outlined. You may well have to rethink and reassess much of what your old *belief systems* have been telling you about what is important in life. In short, you may need to reflect on how and what you think, along with learning to:

\# Begin and end each day in Silence, with Prayer, and with Reflection.

\# Give up a short-term mindset and be patient.

\# Create your very own good **daily habits**.

\# Give up playing small, be Responsible and take Ownership of YOUR life.

\# Give up excuses and live 'Above the Line.' (i.e. be a **Master Achiever**).

\# Stay away from negative, emotionally-draining people and stop trying to please everyone.

\# Tame your mind so that you can control your Ego.

What is essential now, to take full advantage of what this book can do for you, is to slowly *RE-READ* it as soon as possible. This time using a highlighter pen (if you haven't already done so) and highlight the sentences and sections all the way through the book that stand-out for you. <u>This

<u>is very important</u>. It is the exact practice that I have adopted myself whenever I read a self-help or spiritual book.

The structure of this book has been designed with the aim that you will regularly refer to it, thus ensuring that you constantly practise adopting this life-changing strategy of **LOOKING WITHIN** when faced with many of the issues that you are confronted with <u>daily</u>. Refer regularly to those pages with the **LARGE BOLD PRINT,** as these are a quick and easy reference with simple, powerful messages.

N.B: Always carry something inspirational to read *e.g. this book!*

The idea now is to **NOT** just put this book away on a bookshelf or place it in a desk drawer, or onto a shelf, as the book has been written with the aim that you would carry it with you **daily,** in a briefcase, a backpack, a handbag, or place it on your office desk so you can refer to it regularly like any book of learning, just as you would have done when studying at school or university. This is a textbook on Life, on how to grow and develop spiritually (remember Body, Mind, & Spirit) which is essential for living a fulfilled and worthwhile life. It is a practical guide book on 'how to' manifest **lasting happiness, inner peace and contentment** in your everyday living!

It is also important that you now immediately start to find a 'quiet space', and a specific time of day, to **DAILY** recite/whisper the Prayers, the **daily** Rules and the Abundance Affirmation in Chapter 7, together with the extra Affirmations and the Teachings of Buddha in Chapter 8. Choose those affirmations that resonate with you, that are **'lightbulbs'** for you if you like, type them up and place them where you can see them regularly — at least **daily!**

Take the Chapter 9 chart on *'Master Achievers and Victims'*, type it up on A4 size paper, have it laminated and place a copy on your refrigerator or pantry door so that your family and friends can refer to it. Then have everyone in your household accountable for what they say and do. This is a very powerful life-changing practise to adopt, and you can have a lot of fun with it, particularly when young children may refer you to it after you said or did something where your initial response may have you performing below the line! Maybe you could have a 'Below the Line' jar, where if someone within your household or workplace is caught-out speaking or acting 'below the line', then they must pay a small fine of $1 for example into that jar. You can have fun with this exercise, while at the same time everyone learns a valuable lesson.

Start every day with a **GRATITUDE ATTACK.** Go out and buy a **Gratitude Journal,** or any type of book with blank pages, and just date the pages as you go. Start writing in it at least five things that YOU are grateful for **DAILY!** Maybe you could start with being grateful that you have a pulse, or that you have read this book and are now adopting the practices as outlined within these pages! Maybe you are grateful that you woke up and have once again been offered the 'special gift' of another day of living, a new day to work at fulfilling your dreams, to make more mistakes and to learn from them, etc.

Maybe you are grateful for another 'blank page' to write the next chapter in the story of YOUR LIFE and for a new day to be of 'service'. Maybe you are grateful that you can shower/bath/clean your teeth, etc. in clean running hot and cold water. Perhaps, you are grateful that you have now learnt how vital being **aware** of all of this is to manifesting <u>lasting</u> **happiness, inner peace and contentment** in YOUR life! Allow your 'Inner Self' to reveal a whole lot more to be grateful for, as showing gratitude <u>daily</u> is open, honest participation in YOUR life, which is your spirituality. Concentrate, be disciplined, always be present, and continually **Look Within!**

STOP, PAUSE, REFLECT and **LISTEN** to the messages that you are receiving as you have been reading this book. Being present to every moment in your life is living it. Be more **aware,** for being

Look Within

aware is wisdom in action! Always pay attention to all that is around you, and you cannot do that if you are not living in the present moment. *Get out of the Ego and get into Spirit.* Don't be filled with negative thoughts of guilt, fear, anger or jealousy. And always see the love and innocence in all mankind behind the masks that we all wear, and the illusions of this worldly plane.

Most of all, strive to:

Love what YOU think. Love what YOU say. Love what YOU do.

In other words, *LOVE YOU.*

Be Inspired   Be Astonished   Be Excited   Be Amazed   Be ALIVE!

Life is short, so one needs to:

*Laugh often.

*Apologise when you should.

*'Let Go' of what you cannot control or change e.g. the past!

*Give everything you have LIVING each day and having no regrets.

*Take time out to be Grateful, to recharge Body, Mind & Spirit - **DAILY**

*Take the good with the bad.

*And always, say **THANK YOU!**

When these two words, **THANK YOU,** become second nature to you, and you are consciously aware that you are regularly expressing them for all sorts of reasons as you go about your day, then you will become **aware** of how powerful these two precious words truly are. Together with the positive effect they have on your physical and mental wellbeing, and on that of others with whom you have contact! If in doubt, just try doing it for a week or two. You will be amazed. **Thank You!**

'God, as I live each day, walk with me along the way.

Today I'm sure I need you near to give me strength and to wipe out fear.

By myself, I would never cope, but in your spirit lies my hope.

So, I ask for your power, as I face this very hour.'

(Author Unknown)

WHEN WE STOP LISTENING, WE STOP LEARNING.

WE THEN LOSE OUR GRASP ON WHAT MATTERS!

<u>Remember:</u> THE EGO IS ALWAYS YOUR ENEMY!

Conclusion

'It matters little what others say and think of me, it matters much what I say and think of myself.'
– (Oscar Wilde)

This statement has been *THE* single most powerful **awakening** quote that I have ever read, and subsequently adopted as a part of my belief system and hence my <u>daily</u> living! If you, the reader of this book, have the same **'lightbulb'** moment as I did when you first read this quote, and you too then draw on it extensively in your life, as I have and still do, then my job as the author of this book will have been a tremendous success and I will be eternally grateful. Grateful that I may have played a small part in **awakening** another person somewhere in the world to the power of living their life by learning the enormous benefits of **LOOKING WITHIN, <u>daily</u>**. I hope the readers of this book will begin travelling on their very own journey, not worrying what others may say or think of them, but rather, living their life pursuing their dreams and plans in accordance with their very own strongly held Beliefs & Faith. i.e. *following the whispers of their heart!*

Awaken today to the reality of your 'Inner Life' and be in tune with all that comes with it. If possible, regularly walk alone in nature and feel the energy that resides within that magnificent silent space, for it is within moments like this that you will feel connected to that world of 'gifts' that I have spoken about and for which we often take for granted. For example, the simple 'gifts' of breathing, of being able to move freely, to see and hear clearly, to hear and smell the rain, view sunrises and sunsets, etc, etc.

Ask God/Spirit/Source/? to **awaken** your senses <u>daily</u> so that you can acknowledge, accept, and be grateful <u>daily</u> for these wonderful gifts and much, much more. Don't be overly impressed by money, degrees, titles, Facebook fans/likes, looks, body image, etc. none of which guarantees happiness. But rather, be inspired by Kindness, Gratefulness, Honesty, Compassion, Integrity, Forgiveness, Humility, Generosity and Love for all, *including Yourself!*

Life is not about being famous, being popular, being rich, being attractive, being highly educated

Conclusion

or being perfect (no such thing!). Life IS about *listening to those whispers of your heart*, being authentic, being inspired, being grateful, being truthful, being non-judgemental, being humble, being kind and compassionate towards others, particularly the less fortunate.

Take a chance. Life has no guarantees! If you spend your life waiting for guarantees then you may well be waiting a very long time, and life may just pass you by. Whatever it is that you choose to do with your life, ensure that you **DO NO HARM**. Believe in yourself, follow your heart rather than your head or the opinion of others, and live your truth. Have enormous courage and push through thoughts that hold you back. Release your fears and trust that your needs, not necessarily your wants, will always be met in accordance with **God's Master Plan** (Chapter 3). Invest in yourself, because YOU are the best investment that you will ever have!

- Read good books.
- Sit often in silence and meditate.
- Eat healthy, wholesome food.
- Move or exercise.
- Spend time in nature.
- Live and Let Live.
- Rest.

Start a **daily ritual/practise.** Apply now what you have learned from reading this book. If not, then ask yourself: **'If not now, then when?**

Learn from All. Judge No-one. Be Kind to All. And always, always, say: **Thank You!**

Do not take life too seriously. At the end of the day, you must be able to laugh at yourself, 'let go' of anger, and practise the four L's: **LIVE – LOVE – LAUGH – LOTS!** In everything that you do, be Gentle, be Kind, be Wise, be Thoughtful, be Honest, be Compassionate, be Loving, be Fair, be Reasonable and be Generous to All – including to Yourself! And remember, you always have a choice in everything that you Think, Say and Do! Being able to choose is personal power. Choose to grow and evolve in YOUR life, always strive to do your very best, and have no regrets!

You should by now have a greater **awareness** of how your Attachments and Beliefs have created your Reality, your current thinking, and how you speak and act, etc. Now that you have read this book, YOU are the one who has the 'power to choose'. You can choose to say "Yes, I agree", or you can choose to say 'No, I do not agree with the messages that I have read throughout this book". That choice is yours and yours alone! That, my friend, is true Freedom. It is the freedom to choose, the freedom to live your Truth, and the freedom to live your Purpose!

Conclusion

My request of you now is that, as a bare minimum, you begin every day with an open mind and heart. I request that you think deeply and honestly on what you have read in these pages. I further request that you place the book somewhere that you will regularly see it, pick it up, and re-read from it from time to time, to reinforce in *your mind* the legitimacy of your changing Beliefs.

Be gentle with yourself, be courageous, be patient, be committed, be disciplined, and you will become **aware** of the benefits that **Looking Within** has on your 'Inner Self', on your Soul! You cannot unread what you have read in this book. Ultimately, if you choose to focus and persist **DAILY,** and adopt the **daily habits** that I have outlined in detail throughout the book, then you too will subtly discover this same simple pathway to achieving **lasting happiness, inner peace and contentment** in YOUR life.

Do not expect things to change immediately. Positive change, as I have said earlier, can initially be challenging, confronting, uncomfortable, and often evolve slowly. It takes time and commitment to embrace these **daily habits**/practises and to change your current behaviour patterns and beliefs, so be patient and gentle with yourself. Simply have faith and trust that **awareness/wisdom** evolves through your challenges! We all need to have challenges in life. May you enjoy the magical journey of living YOUR LIFE the way that YOU want to live it. God bless you, my friend, and remember to always **Look Within** for that inner peace and contentment that we all desire. It resides within each of us, and you too are now **aware** that you need only **Look Within** to discover it and to embrace it too!

> **'After all, it is those who have a deep and real inner life who are best able to deal with the irritating details of the outer life.'**
> **– (Evelyn Underhill)**

> **'Whatsoever you can do, or dream you can, begin it. Boldness has genius, power and magic in it.'**
> **– (Johann Wolfgang von Goethe)**

Let me conclude with firstly an assertion from the Buddha, followed by a powerful prayer courtesy from 'A Course in Miracles', and finally, a favourite poem of mine titled 'Footprints'.

These are offered to demonstrate to you that you **NEVER** need to walk alone on your life's journey.

Buddha

The thought manifests as the word;

The word manifests as the deed;

The deed develops into **habit;**

A **habit** hardens into character.

So, watch the thought and its ways with care;

And let it spring from love born out of concern for all beings.

As the shadow follows the body;

As we think, so we become.

The Prayer

Let us be still an instant, and forget
all things we ever learned, all thoughts we had
and every preconception that we hold
of what things mean and what their purpose is.
Let us remember not our own ideas of what the world is for.
We do not know.
Let every image held of everyone
be loosened from our minds and swept away.
Be innocent of judgement
unaware of any thoughts of evil or of good

Look Within

that ever crossed your mind of anyone.
Now, do you know Him not.
But you are free to learn of Him
and learn of Him anew.
Only be quiet.
You will need no rule but this
to let your practising today
lift you above the thinking of the world
and free your vision from the body's eyes.
Only be still and listen. Simply do this.
Be still, and lay aside all thoughts
of what you are and what God is,
all concepts you have learned about the world,
all images you hold about yourself.
Empty your mind of everything
it thinks is either true or false,
or good or bad,
of every thought it judges worthy
and all ideas of which it is ashamed.
Hold onto nothing.
Do not bring with you one thought
the past has taught, nor one belief
you ever learned before from anything.
Forget this world
and come with wholly empty hands unto <u>your</u> God.

Conclusion

The Poem

FOOTPRINTS

One night a man had a dream. He dreamt that he was walking along a beach with the Lord. Across the sky flashed scenes from his life. For each scene, he noticed two sets of footprints in the sand, one belonging to him and the other to the Lord.

When the last scene of his life flashed before him, he looked back at the footprints in the sand. He noticed that many times along the path of his life there was only one set of footprints. He also noticed that this happened at the very lowest and saddest times in his life.

This really bothered him, and so he questioned the Lord about it.

"Lord, you said that once I decided to follow you, you'd walk with me all the way. But I have noticed during the more troublesome times in my life there is only one set of footprints. I don't understand why when I needed you most you would leave me."

The Lord replied, "My son, my precious child, I love you and would never leave you. During your times of trial and suffering, when you see only one set of footprints, it was then that I carried you."

(Author Unknown)

Finally, regardless of what you or I do in this life, in three words, I can sum up the ultimate reality that I have learned about life: **IT GOES ON!**

Let me give you a personal example of becoming **aware** of this fact. Some years ago, whilst my wife and I were holidaying on Norfolk Island, we took some time to visit a garden nursery, because as I wrote earlier my wife is an avid gardener. Whilst Liz walked through this garden admiring the plant life and chatting with the business owner about plants (as you do!), I sat on a seat that had been built around the base of this magnificent, huge, very healthy tree that was situated inside the boundary of the nursey, and that looked out across and down to the ocean and a glorious beach below.

The circumference of the base of this tree was at least ten metres, and the trunk reached straight upward towards the sky. This tree was huge! When my wife had completed her chat, I asked the nursery owner if she had any idea as to the age of this magnificent specimen of a tree. Her reply was that she had been advised that it was estimated this tree was some 600-800 years old! It was at that very moment that I became **aware** that we humans, individually at least, are completely insignificant to Mother Earth. We are lucky to survive 10% of the time this and many other trees survive on this planet. We as individuals come and go rather quickly in comparison to many of these magnificent trees which can survive for hundreds of years. It was a stark reminder of how insignificant and unimportant we humans are to the wonderful world of nature. We are, each of us, but a short blip in time.

<u>Moral of this short story:</u> **Make the most of every day that you have! Your life-clock is ticking. Tick-tock, tick-tock, tick-tock, tick-tock……**

Resources

For further resources on the power of learning the skill of **Looking Within** visit:

www.lookwithin.com.au

and/or

www.gerrydoes.com.au

Acknowledgements

I want to express my heartfelt thanks and gratitude to my beautiful wife Liz for her love and unending support through this often rather stressful but also rewarding experience of writing and producing a book that one hopes will have a positive impact on the lives of many.

I also want to acknowledge and express my gratitude to the many wonderful authors and mentors, particularly those listed below, who have contributed to my life-long and on-going journey of spiritual discovery/**awakening**. And it is so true that they all express this same sentiment: **one should never stop learning!** Thank you all so much.

Furthermore, I wish to make special mention of Emily Gowor who is the person ultimately responsible for transcribing my work into print through Gowor International Publishers. Thank you, Emily, for your guidance, coaching, encouragement, support, and for your ongoing belief in me to be able to produce this book! You definitely are one of God's 'Earth Angels'!

I highly recommend to you this group of wonderful teachers/mentors for further reference from their books, YouTube videos, etc.:

Dr Wayne Dyer
Marianne Williamson
Lama Surya Das
Sarah Ban Breathnach
Emily Gowor
Thich Nat Hanh
Don Miguel Ruiz
The Dalai Lama
Joan Boysen
Bronnie Ware
Doreen Virtue
Deepak Chopra
Neale Donald Walsh
Gabrielle Bernstein
Nair Anastasia
Victor M B Parachi

And I give a further 'special' **Thank You** to News Limited, the company responsible for the photo that I have incorporated at the front of the book.

About the Author

Gerry Gleeson was born in the city of Bendigo in central Victoria, Australia. He studied accountancy at university which led to him initially working for an international accountancy firm in Melbourne, Australia, as an auditor. Gerry quickly realised (became **aware!**) that he was not suited to working in an office environment for 8 hours every working day for the rest of his life, so after only one year working as an auditor Gerry quit this office environment, and with a couple of university mates he travelled to the other side of Australia, Western Australia. Here he worked firstly in Hotel/Motel Management in very large hotels for a couple of years, and then moved into the Mining industry again in Western Australia.

It was during this time, thousands of kilometres away from family, that Gerry began to 'let go' of religion in that traditional sense of having to attend church every Sunday. He was becoming **aware** that it was okay not to attend church now that he was away from the traditional family environment, where attending a Sunday mass had been the norm all the way through his life to this point. He became **aware** that you could communicate directly with God at any time, 24/7, regardless of where you lived or worked. Gerry also now realised (became **aware**) for the first time, that it was possible to develop his own beliefs about life and not to just accept living his life based on the beliefs of others (i.e. his parents, teachers, the church, etc.)

For Gerry, this truly was his first experience with the freedom of choice. The freedom to make one's own choices about right and wrong, how to build meaningful relationships, who to learn from, to be personally responsible for his own life, to choose his own mentors and what was important in life and what was not, to not take life for granted, etc. Gerry ultimately moved on from working in the mining sector, spending some years in real estate sales and management in South East Queensland, Australia before he and his future wife Liz invested their life savings in purchasing and successfully operating an accommodation business in Byron Bay, Australia, for a period of some 13 years, where he and Liz still happily reside.

Gerry has always had an intense interest in people and how we all interact, and it was during those

About the Author

13 years of **daily** dealing with the public from all walks of life, that he developed a keen interest in 'spirituality', Buddhism, etc. Subsequently, he read and studied widely on these subjects. It was also during this period of his life that he became **aware** that far too many of us neglect a vital part of who we are (Body/Mind/Spirit) as many spend time concentrating on the Body and the Mind, but little if any time nurturing their Spirit. It is a belief similarly shared by many spiritual/inspirational authors/mentors that Gerry has advocated throughout this book.

Thus, to manifest **lasting happiness, inner peace and contentment** into one's life, then one must learn the importance of developing the **daily** practice of **LOOKING WITHIN!** The secrets to living a happy and contented life are deep within each of us. And to this day Gerry lives by the following quote which he has expressed numerous times throughout the book:

IT MATTERS LITTLE WHAT OTHERS SAY OR THINK OF ME, IT MATTERS MUCH WHAT I SAY AND THINK OF MYSELF.

www.ingramcontent.com/pod-product-compliance
Lightning Source LLC
Chambersburg PA
CBHW071907290426
44110CB00013B/1317